THE SCENIC ROUTE TO SPIRITUALITY

101 (Not So) Serious Paths to Spiritual Enlightenment

Topher Cava

CONTENTS

INTRODUCTION

So you want to be more spiritual? Of course you do. That's why you're here. Well, welcome to the whimsical world of spiritual enlightenment, where laughter is the best path to inner peace! In this delightful guide, you'll embark on a joyous journey filled with 101 not-so-serious ways to elevate your spirit and tickle your funny bone.

These light-hearted practices will show you that spirituality doesn't have to be solemn—it can be downright hilarious! So, sit back, relax, and get ready to laugh your way to enlightenment. After all, who says the path to inner peace can't be paved with laughter?

Let's face it, life can be a rollercoaster of chaos and confusion, like trying to assemble IKEA furniture without the instructions. That's where spirituality swoops in like a superhero in yoga pants. It's like having your own personal GPS for the soul, guiding you through the crazy twists and turns of existence. Sure, it might sound a bit woo-woo, but hey, sometimes you need a little woo-woo to navigate this wild ride called life. So, embrace your inner zen master, because in this crazy world, a little spiritual sanity might just be the ultimate life hack!

MEDITATE LIKE A PRO

or at Least a Procrastinator

P icture this: you're sitting cross-legged on a cushion, eyes closed, trying to "quiet your mind and connect with your inner self." Sounds peaceful, right? Well, welcome to the world of meditation, where your inner self is often more like a mischievous monkey on a caffeine high.

The Setup

You've read all the self-help books, watched those serene meditation videos on YouTube, and even splurged on a fancy meditation app. You're ready to embark on your journey to enlightenment. You light some incense, put on your most comfortable yoga pants (that have definitely never seen the inside of a yoga studio), and assume the lotus position. You're officially in the zone.

The Inner Monologue

As you close your eyes, you're immediately bombarded with thoughts. Did you remember to turn off the stove? What's that weird noise coming from the neighbor's yard? Should you have gone for the organic avocados instead of the regular ones? Your inner monologue is in overdrive, and it's not exactly chanting "om."

The Distractions

Just when you think you're getting the hang of it, a fly decides to buzz right by your ear. You try to ignore it, but it's like a tiny, annoying meditation coach reminding you to stay present. Then there's the itch on your nose that refuses to go away. You resist the urge to scratch, but now your nose feels like it's staging a rebellion against your peaceful intentions.

The Time Warp

You swear it's been at least 20 minutes since you started, but when you peek at the timer on your phone, it's only been three. Time has slowed down to a snail's pace, and you start to wonder if you accidentally stumbled into a wormhole instead of achieving inner peace.

The Epiphany

Just as you're about to give up and reach for your phone to check Instagram (because, let's be real, that's where all the real enlightenment happens), something miraculous happens. You catch a glimpse of stillness amidst the chaos. Maybe it's the way the sunlight filters through the window, or maybe it's just the sheer exhaustion from trying to silence your mind, but you feel a moment of clarity.

The Aftermath

You slowly open your eyes, feeling oddly refreshed and surprisingly zen. Sure, you didn't achieve instant enlightenment, but you did survive a session of meditation without losing your mind (or at least not entirely). You might not be a meditation master just yet, but you're definitely on your way. Plus, you've earned yourself some serious bragging rights for attempting to tame your inner monkey.

So, there you have it—meditation, the not-so-serene way. It might not always be a smooth journey to inner peace, but hey, at least you can laugh about it. And who knows? Maybe one day you'll look back on these moments and realize that the real meditation was the friends we made along the way.

THE MINDFUL MISADVENTURES OF A MODERN MULTITASKER

Ah, mindfulness—the art of being present in the moment. Sounds simple enough, right? Well, for the modern multitasker, living in the moment can feel like trying to catch a greased pig at a county fair. Let's take a humorous look at what it's like to practice mindfulness in the midst of daily chaos.

The Morning Rush

You wake up to the sound of your alarm blaring, reminding you that you're already behind schedule. As you stumble out of bed, you mentally run through your to-do list for the day. Breakfast, check. Shower, check. Coffee, double-check. But wait, weren't you supposed to be practicing mindfulness right now? Oops, guess you'll have to try again tomorrow.

The Commute Conundrum

Whether you're stuck in traffic or crammed into a crowded subway car, commuting is the ultimate test of mindfulness. As you sit in bumper-to-bumper traffic, you try to focus on the present moment. But the guy in the next lane is blasting his music so loudly that you can feel the bass in your bones. And is that a pigeon staring at you from the roof of the bus shelter?

You're pretty sure it's plotting something.

The Office Odyssey

You finally make it to work, only to be bombarded by emails, meetings, and deadlines. As you try to juggle multiple tasks at once, you realize that being mindful in the office is like trying to tame a pack of wild squirrels. Just when you think you've got one under control, another one comes flying in from left field.

The Lunchtime Labyrinth

Lunchtime should be a moment of respite, a chance to savor your meal and recharge for the afternoon. But in reality, it's a mad dash to the nearest fast-food joint or a hurried affair at your desk. You try to eat mindfully, savoring each bite and appreciating the flavors. But before you know it, your lunch break is over, and you're back to the grind.

The Evening Escape

After a long day of multitasking, you finally have some downtime. You decide to unwind with a good book or a favorite TV show, but your mind keeps wandering back to your never-ending to-do list. You try to focus on the story or the plot twists, but it's like your brain has a mind of its own.

The Bedtime Battle

As you crawl into bed, you vow to practice mindfulness before drifting off to sleep. You close your eyes and take a deep breath, trying to clear your mind. But wait, did you remember to lock the front door? And did you turn off the stove? Suddenly, your mind is racing again, and you wonder if you'll ever truly master the art of living in the moment.

The Moral Of The Story

In a world that's constantly pulling us in a million different directions, practicing mindfulness can feel like trying to swim upstream in a river of distractions. But amidst the chaos and the noise, there are moments of stillness and clarity waiting to be discovered. So, the next time you find yourself struggling to stay present, take a deep breath and remember that even the most mindful moments can be found in the midst of everyday madness.

THE GREAT OUTDOORS

and Other Unnatural Habitats

Nature—the great outdoors, where the air is fresh, the scenery is stunning, and the bugs are, well, everywhere. For the urban dweller, spending time in nature can be a refreshing escape from the concrete jungle. Let's take a humorous look at what it's like to appreciate nature's beauty while navigating its quirks.

The Call Of The Wild

You've decided to embark on a nature adventure, armed with sunscreen, bug spray, and a vague sense of optimism. As you step into the great outdoors, you're immediately greeted by a cacophony of sounds—birds chirping, leaves rustling, and the distant roar of a lawnmower. Ah, the serenity of nature.

The Scenic Route

You set off on a picturesque trail, eager to soak in the beauty of your surroundings. The trees tower overhead, casting dappled shadows on the path. You take a deep breath of fresh air, only to inhale a cloud of gnats. Nature's perfume, you tell yourself.

The Wildlife Encounter

As you walk along, you spot a majestic deer grazing in a clearing. You freeze, trying to capture the moment, but your camera decides to focus on a particularly photogenic rock instead. The deer gives you a disdainful look before sauntering off into the woods. You're pretty sure it was laughing at you.

The Grounding Experience

You find a peaceful spot by a babbling brook and decide to sit for a while, feeling nature's grounding energy. You close your eyes and try to connect with the earth beneath you. Just as you start to feel a sense of calm, a mosquito decides to make you its next meal. Grounding, indeed.

The Nature's Gym

You come across a steep hill and decide to climb it for a better view. Halfway up, you realize that hiking is nature's way of reminding you that the gym exists for a reason. Your legs burn, your lungs protest, and you start to question your life choices. But hey, at least the view is worth it.

The Picnic Perils

You decide to have a picnic to fully embrace the outdoor experience. As you unpack your sandwiches and snacks, you're immediately surrounded by a squadron of ants. They seem to have mistaken your picnic blanket for an all-you-can-eat buffet. You contemplate sharing your meal with them but decide against it.

The Nature's Finale

As the day draws to a close, you watch the sunset, its golden rays painting the sky in a breathtaking display. You feel a sense of awe and wonder, forgetting the bugs, the hills, and the ants for a moment. Nature's beauty is undeniable, even if it comes with a few quirks.

The Moral Of The Story

Nature has a way of humbling us, reminding us that we're just small specks in a vast and wondrous world. So, the next time you venture into the great outdoors, embrace its quirks, laugh at its surprises, and take in its beauty. After all, nature's sense of humor is as wild as it gets.

THE GRATITUDE JOURNAL CHRONICLES

A Comedy of Thankfulness

Keeping a gratitude journal sounds like a simple and wholesome activity—just jot down a few things you're thankful for each day, right? Well, as with many things in life, the reality can be a bit more... entertaining. Join us on a whimsical journey through the world of gratitude journaling.

The Pledge

You've decided to start a gratitude journal to cultivate a sense of appreciation for the blessings in your life. Armed with a new notebook and a pen (or maybe just your phone's notes app), you're ready to embark on this journey of thankfulness. You take a deep breath and begin your first entry.

Day 1: A Comedy Of Errors

You sit down to write in your gratitude journal, but your pen runs out of ink after the first word. No worries, you grab another pen, only to find that it's out of ink too. Finally, you resort to typing on your phone, but autocorrect has other plans. "I'm grateful for my job" becomes "I'm grateful for my slob," and you can't help but laugh at the absurdity of it all.

Day 5: The Struggle Is Real

You're starting to get the hang of this gratitude thing. You jot down things like "a sunny day" and "a good cup of coffee," feeling pretty proud of yourself. But then you start to worry that your entries are too mundane. Are you supposed to be grateful for more profound things? Like world peace or discovering a new planet? You decide to stick with the small stuff for now.Day 10: The Great Revelation

As you write in your journal, you have a sudden epiphany. You realize that gratitude isn't just about the big, life-changing moments. It's about finding joy in the little things, like a warm hug or a funny meme. You chuckle to yourself as you write, grateful for the clarity that comes with a few weeks of journaling.

Day 15: The Gratitude Challenge

You've been challenged to find 10 things you're grateful for each day. At first, you balk at the idea—10 things? That's a lot of things! But as you start listing them out, you realize that gratitude is like a muscle that gets stronger with exercise. You might not be able to bench press a car, but you can certainly flex your gratitude muscles.

Day 20: The Gratitude High

You're on a roll now. Your gratitude journal is filled with entries about everything from your morning cup of tea to the kindness of strangers. You're starting to see the world through a different lens, one that's tinted with appreciation and wonder. Who knew that a simple journal could have such a profound effect?

The Moral Of The Story

Keeping a gratitude journal may seem like a small and simple act, but its impact can be profound. It's a reminder to find joy in the everyday moments, to appreciate the things we often take for granted, and to laugh at life's little quirks along the way. So, grab a pen (or your phone) and start jotting down those thankful thoughts. Who knows what comedic gems you'll uncover in the process?

YOGA, TAI CHI, AND THE QUEST FOR INNER HARMONY

I n the quest for balance and harmony, many turn to the ancient practices of yoga and tai chi. These disciplines promise to harmonize body, mind, and spirit, but for the uninitiated, they can be a journey into the unknown. Join us as we embark on a humorous exploration of yoga, tai chi, and the pursuit of inner peace.

The Yoga Studio Odyssey

You enter the yoga studio, feeling a mix of excitement and trepidation. The room is filled with serene music and the sound of gentle breathing. You unroll your mat and try to strike a pose that vaguely resembles what the instructor is demonstrating. As you attempt to contort your body into impossible shapes, you wonder if you've accidentally stumbled into a modern-day circus.

The Warrior Pose Dilemma

You're in the middle of a challenging yoga class, trying to hold a warrior pose without toppling over. Your muscles are shaking, and sweat is pouring down your face. Just as you're about to give up and collapse into a heap, the instructor tells you to smile and breathe deeply. You're pretty sure they're secretly a sadist.

The Downward Dog Debacle

You're instructed to move into downward dog, a seemingly simple pose that feels anything but. As you attempt to align your body in the right angles, you realize that your dog would be ashamed of your lack of flexibility. You try to focus on your breath, but all you can think about is how much you miss your couch.

The Tai Chi Tango

In the world of tai chi, slow and steady wins the race. You move through a series of graceful, flowing movements, trying to emulate the instructor's serene demeanor. But as you attempt to coordinate your breath with your movements, you feel more like a clumsy dancer than a master of martial arts. You hope no one is watching.

The Harmony Hurdles

As you continue your practice, you start to feel a sense of calm and centeredness wash over you. You realize that yoga and tai chi are not just physical exercises but pathways to inner peace. Sure, you might wobble in tree pose or forget the next tai chi sequence, but you're learning to embrace the journey, warts and all.

The Inner Harmony

As you roll up your mat and leave the studio, you feel a newfound sense of balance and clarity. The world seems a little bit brighter, and your troubles a little bit smaller. You realize that yoga and tai chi are not just about perfecting poses or movements but about finding harmony within yourself.

The Moral Of The Story

Yoga and tai chi may have their challenges, but they also offer a path to inner harmony and well-being. Whether you're a seasoned practitioner or a complete newbie, the journey to balance and peace is always worth the effort. So, roll out your mat, take a deep breath, and embrace the adventure that awaits on the path to harmony.

THE VOLUNTEER CHRONICLES

A Humorous Quest for Purpose

Volunteering for a cause you believe in can be a noble and fulfilling endeavor. It promises to connect you to a larger purpose and make a positive impact on the world. But as with any adventure, there are bound to be some unexpected twists and turns along the way. Join us as we embark on a humorous journey through the world of volunteering.

The Noble Intentions

You've decided to volunteer for a cause close to your heart. Armed with enthusiasm and a desire to make a difference, you sign up for your first volunteer gig. You imagine yourself changing the world, one act of kindness at a time. Little do you know, the world has other plans.

The Orientation Odyssey

You arrive at the volunteer orientation, eager to learn about your role and how you can contribute. But as the presenter drones on about policies and procedures, you start to wonder if you accidentally wandered into a corporate training seminar. You're pretty sure you didn't sign up for this level of bureaucracy.

The Team-Building Tango

You're assigned to a team of fellow volunteers, each with their own quirks and personalities. As you attempt to bond with your newfound comrades, you realize that teamwork is a lot like herding cats—chaotic, unpredictable, and occasionally scratchy. But hey, at least you're in it together, right?

The Task Tumble

You're given your first assignment, and it's not exactly what you had in mind. Instead of saving the world, you find yourself sorting through a mountain of paperwork or scrubbing toilets at the local shelter. You start to wonder if this is what they meant by "making a difference." Nevertheless, you soldier on, determined to find purpose in even the most mundane tasks.

The Unexpected Lessons

As you continue your volunteer work, you start to notice unexpected changes within yourself. You feel a sense of fulfillment and purpose that you didn't expect. You realize that making a difference isn't always about grand gestures—it's about showing up, putting in the effort, and being present for those who need it most.

The Community Connection

As you become more involved in your volunteer work, you start to feel a sense of belonging within the community. You forge friendships with your fellow volunteers and the people you're serving. You realize that the true magic of volunteering lies in the connections you make and the lives you touch along the way.

The Moral Of The Story

Volunteering is not just about giving your time and effort—it's about being open to the unexpected, embracing the challenges, and finding joy in the journey. Whether you're sorting through paperwork or changing the world one toilet at a time, your efforts are making a difference. So, keep volunteering, keep laughing, and keep making the world a better place—one comedic adventure at a time.

THE SPIRITUAL QUEST
FOR ENLIGHTENMENT

with a Side of Laughter

R eading spiritual books or listening to inspiring lectures can be a transformative experience, promising enlightenment and personal growth. But let's face it— sometimes the journey to spiritual enlightenment is paved with unexpected detours and comedic mishaps. Join us as we embark on a humorous exploration of the world of spiritual literature and lectures.

The Bookstore Odyssey

You enter the bookstore with a sense of purpose, determined to find the perfect spiritual book that will unlock the secrets of the universe. As you peruse the shelves, you're overwhelmed by the sheer number of titles promising enlightenment in 10 easy steps or less. You wonder if there's a "Cliff's Notes" version for spiritual awakening.

The Self-Help Shuffle

You finally settle on a book that speaks to your soul, filled with promises of inner peace and boundless joy. You eagerly dive into the first chapter, only to be greeted by a barrage of unfamiliar terms and concepts. You find yourself Googling words like "chakra" and "karma," wondering if you accidentally stumbled into a foreign language class.

The Lecture Limbo

You decide to attend a spiritual lecture by a renowned guru, hoping to gain some wisdom and insight. As you sit in the audience, you're struck by the guru's serene presence and wise words. But just as you start to feel a sense of enlightenment wash over you, your stomach decides to join the conversation with an untimely rumble. You try to disguise it as a meditative mantra, but the guy next to you gives you a strange look.

The Inner Dialogue Dilemma

You're halfway through a particularly profound passage in your spiritual book when your inner skeptic decides to chime in. "Is this really going to change your life?" it asks. "Maybe you should just stick to Netflix." You try to silence the voice of doubt, but it's like a relentless heckler at a stand-up comedy show.

The Epiphany (Or Lack Thereof)

As you reach the end of your book or lecture, you're filled with a sense of anticipation. This is it—the moment of enlightenment you've been waiting for. But as you close the book or the lecture ends, you're left feeling... well, pretty much the same as before. You wonder if you missed something or if enlightenment got lost in the mail.

The Moral Of The Story

Embarking on a spiritual journey can be both enlightening and entertaining. Whether you're reading about ancient wisdom or listening to modern gurus, remember to approach it with an open mind and a sense of humor. After all, laughter is often the best path to enlightenment. So, keep reading, keep listening, and keep laughing your way to spiritual growth.

THE FORGIVENESS FOLLIES

An Amusing Guide to Letting Go

Forgiveness—it's a noble act that promises to free us from the burden of resentment and cultivate compassion. But let's be real, forgiveness is easier said than done, especially when you're trying to navigate the minefield of human emotions. Join us as we embark on a humorous exploration of the art of forgiveness and the comedic mishaps that often accompany it.

The Resentment Rodeo

You find yourself holding onto a grudge tighter than a squirrel hoarding nuts for winter. Every time you think about the person who wronged you, you feel a surge of righteous indignation. You're pretty sure you could win a gold medal in the Olympic sport of holding onto resentments.

The Forgiveness Fumble

You decide it's time to let go of your resentment and practice forgiveness. You take a deep breath and try to summon feelings of compassion. But just as you're about to forgive, your inner voice decides to chime in with a laundry list of reasons why you shouldn't. You're pretty sure your inner voice is a stand-up comedian in disguise.

The Compassion Conundrum

You attempt to cultivate compassion for the person who wronged you, but it feels like trying to hug a cactus. Every time you think you've found a shred of empathy, it's quickly overshadowed by a prickly reminder of why you're mad in the first place. You wonder if compassion is hiding in a secret compartment somewhere.

The Letting Go Limbo

You're trying to let go of your resentment, but it's like trying to wrangle a greased pig at a county fair. Just when you think you've got a hold on it, it slips right through your fingers and you're back to square one. You start to wonder if you'll ever master the art of letting go.

The Epiphany (Or Lack Thereof... Again)

After much soul-searching and inner turmoil, you finally reach a moment of clarity. You realize that forgiveness isn't about letting go of your anger—it's about acknowledging it and choosing to move forward anyway. You might not have a sudden burst of compassion, but you do have a newfound sense of acceptance. And maybe, just maybe, that's enough.

The Moral Of The Story

Forgiveness is a messy, complicated, and often comedic journey. It's not about flipping a switch and suddenly feeling all warm and fuzzy inside. It's about embracing the messiness of human emotions, acknowledging your own shortcomings, and choosing to move forward with an open heart and a sense of humor. So, the next time you find yourself grappling with forgiveness, remember to laugh at the absurdity of it all. After all, forgiveness is a lot like a good joke—it's best when it comes from the heart.

THE KINDNESS CONUNDRUM

A Witty Guide to Spreading Joy

E ngaging in acts of kindness towards others is a noble pursuit that promises to foster a sense of interconnectedness and spread joy. But let's face it—being kind in a world that sometimes feels like a comedy of errors can be a bit of a challenge. Join us as we embark on a humorous exploration of the art of kindness and the comedic twists and turns that come with it.

The Kindness Quest

You embark on a mission to spread kindness, armed with good intentions and a smile. You start small, holding the door open for someone or letting a car merge in front of you in traffic. You feel like a modern-day superhero, fighting the forces of grumpiness and indifference.

The Random Acts Of Chaos

You decide to up your kindness game and perform some random acts of kindness. You pay for the coffee of the person behind you in line, only to realize that they ordered the most expensive drink on the menu. You smile and wave as you drive away, secretly hoping they didn't order a dozen more for their office.

The Kindness Catastrophe

You attempt a grand gesture of kindness, like organizing a charity event or volunteering at a homeless shelter. As you navigate the logistics and details, you realize that kindness is a lot like herding cats—chaotic, unpredictable, and occasionally scratchy. But hey, at least you're making a difference, even if it feels like herding cats.

The Kindness Karma

As you continue to spread kindness, you start to notice unexpected changes within yourself. You feel a sense of joy and fulfillment that you didn't expect. You realize that kindness isn't just about helping others—it's about connecting with them on a deeper level and experiencing the joy of giving.

The Kindness Comedy

You encounter some comedic mishaps along the way, like accidentally complimenting someone's pregnancy when they're not pregnant or offering a high-five to someone who was just waving to a friend behind you. You learn to laugh at these moments and embrace the unexpected twists and turns of kindness.

The Moral Of The Story

Spreading kindness is a noble pursuit that promises to connect us to others and spread joy. It might not always go according to plan, and there might be some comedic mishaps along the way, but the impact of kindness is undeniable. So, keep spreading joy, keep laughing, and keep making the world a little bit brighter—

one act of kindness at a time.

THE QUEST FOR LIFE'S PURPOSE

A Lighthearted Guide to Finding Your Path

Reflecting on your life purpose and aligning your actions with it is a profound and meaningful endeavor. But let's be real—figuring out your life's purpose can feel a bit like trying to solve a Rubik's Cube blindfolded. Join us as we embark on a humorous exploration of the quest for life's purpose and the comedic twists and turns that come with it.

The Existential Crisis

You find yourself pondering the big questions of life—Why am I here? What is my purpose? Is there such a thing as too much pizza? You start to wonder if you missed the memo on life's purpose or if it got lost in the junk mail.

The Soul-Searching Safari

You embark on a soul-searching journey, hoping to uncover the secrets of your life's purpose. You try meditation, journaling, and maybe even a vision quest or two. But just as you're about to have a breakthrough, your stomach decides to join the conversation with an untimely rumble. You wonder if your life's purpose is hiding in the fridge.

The Eureka Moment (Or Lack Thereof)

After much soul-searching and introspection, you finally have a eureka moment. You realize that your purpose in life is... well, still a bit unclear. You're pretty sure it has something to do with making a difference and leaving the world a little bit better than you found it. But the specifics are still a work in progress.

The Action Alignment Shuffle

You decide to align your actions with your newfound sense of purpose. You start making changes in your life, big and small, to reflect your values and goals. But just as you're about to pat yourself on the back, life throws you a curveball, and you're back to square one. You wonder if there's a cosmic game of "whack-a-mole" being played with your life's purpose.

The Purposeful Pursuit

Despite the comedic mishaps and unexpected detours, you continue to pursue your life's purpose with determination and a sense of humor. You realize that the journey is just as important as the destination, and that sometimes, the best discoveries are made when you least expect them.

The Moral Of The Story

Reflecting on your life's purpose is a profound and meaningful journey that promises to bring clarity and direction to your life. It might not always be smooth sailing, and there might be some comedic mishaps along the way, but the quest for purpose is a journey worth taking. So, keep reflecting, keep laughing, and keep searching for your path in this grand comedic adventure called life.

THE AWE AND WONDER EXPEDITION

A Whimsical Adventure in Curiosity

Cultivating a sense of awe and wonder by exploring new ideas and experiences sounds like a grand adventure. But let's face it—sometimes the pursuit of knowledge and discovery can feel a bit like stumbling through a funhouse of mirrors. Join us as we embark on a humorous exploration of the pursuit of awe and wonder and the comedic mishaps that come with it.

The Curiosity Quest

You set out on a quest for knowledge and enlightenment, armed with a sense of wonder and a healthy dose of curiosity. You dive headfirst into new ideas and experiences, eager to expand your mind and broaden your horizons. Little do you know, the universe has some surprises in store for you.

The Intellectual Odyssey

You dive into a book or a lecture on a topic that piques your interest, hoping to unlock the secrets of the universe. But just as you start to feel a spark of understanding, you realize that you're in over your head. You're pretty sure the author is speaking a different language—one that's a cross between ancient Sanskrit and modern-day emoji.

The Philosophical Puzzle

You ponder the big questions of life—What is the meaning of existence? Is there life on other planets? Why do we park in driveways and drive on parkways? You start to wonder if the universe is just one big cosmic joke, and you're the punchline.

The Mindfulness Maze

You attempt to be present and mindful in the moment, hoping to find awe and wonder in the everyday. But just as you start to feel a sense of peace and clarity, your mind decides to join the conversation with a barrage of random thoughts. You try to silence it, but it's like trying to herd cats.

The Epiphany (Or Lack Thereof... Again)

After much intellectual gymnastics and philosophical pondering, you finally have a moment of clarity. You realize that awe and wonder aren't just about finding answers—they're about embracing the questions and marveling at the mysteries of life. You might not have all the answers, but you're okay with that. After all, where's the fun in knowing everything?

The Moral Of The Story

Cultivating a sense of awe and wonder is a lifelong journey that promises to expand your mind and enrich your life. It might not always go according to plan, and there might be some comedic mishaps along the way, but the pursuit of knowledge and discovery is a journey worth taking. So, keep exploring, keep laughing, and keep marveling at the wonders of the universe.

.

THE POSITIVITY PARTY

A Playful Guide to Finding Your Spiritual Squad

Surrounding yourself with positive, uplifting people who support your spiritual growth sounds like a dream come true. But let's face it—building your spiritual squad can feel a bit like trying to assemble a team of superheroes from a group of office workers. Join us as we embark on a humorous exploration of finding your spiritual tribe and the comedic adventures that come with it.

The Squad Search

You set out on a quest to find your spiritual squad, armed with a smile and an open heart. You're on the lookout for people who radiate positivity and uplift your spirits. Little do you know, the universe has a few surprises in store for you.

The Positive Posse

You start to assemble your spiritual squad, gathering friends and acquaintances who share your values and goals. But just as you start to feel like you've found your tribe, someone decides to bring up politics at the dinner table. You try to steer the conversation back to positivity, but it's like trying to herd cats.

The Uplifting Utopia

You imagine your spiritual squad as a group of enlightened beings, sitting in a circle and sharing wisdom and insight. But in reality, it's more like a sitcom with a laugh track. There are moments of profound insight, but they're often overshadowed by comedic mishaps and unexpected twists.

The Support System Shuffle

As you continue to nurture your relationships with your spiritual squad, you start to feel a sense of support and camaraderie. You realize that your squad might not be perfect, but they're there for you when it counts. You're pretty sure that's what friendship is all about—being there for each other, even when life gets a little crazy.

The Epiphany (Or Lack Thereof... Again)

After many laughs and shared moments, you realize that your spiritual squad is more than just a group of friends—they're your support system, your sounding board, and your partners in comedy. You might not have all the answers, but you're okay with that. After all, life is a lot more fun when you're laughing with friends.

The Moral Of The Story

Surrounding yourself with positive, uplifting people is a key ingredient in your spiritual journey. It might not always go according to plan, and there might be some comedic mishaps along the way, but the support and laughter of your spiritual squad make it all worthwhile. So, keep surrounding yourself with positivity, keep laughing, and keep growing with your spiritual squad by your side.

THE QUEST FOR ZEN

An Entertaining Guide to Creating Your Sacred Space

C reating a sacred space in your home where you can meditate or pray sounds like a peaceful endeavor. But let's face it—transforming a corner of your home into a sanctuary of serenity can be a bit like trying to turn a studio apartment into a zen garden. Join us as we embark on a humorous exploration of the quest for creating your sacred space and the comedic mishaps that come with it.

The Sacred Space Saga Begins

You embark on a mission to create your sacred space, armed with candles, incense, and a vague sense of feng shui. You envision a tranquil oasis where you can escape the chaos of daily life and find inner peace. Little do you know, the universe has some surprises in store for you.

The Feng Shui Fiasco

You attempt to arrange your sacred space according to the principles of feng shui, hoping to create a harmonious flow of energy. But just as you start to arrange your furniture, you realize that your room is about as far from feng shui as a clown car at a traffic jam. You wonder if there's a feng shui emergency hotline you can call.

The Decor Dilemma

You start to decorate your sacred space with meaningful objects and symbols that resonate with your spiritual beliefs. But as you start to hang up your tapestries and statues, you realize that your sacred space is starting to look more like a medieval dungeon than a zen retreat. You consider adding a suit of armor for effect.

The Meditation Mayhem

You attempt to meditate in your newly created sacred space, hoping to find peace and tranquility. But just as you close your eyes and start to focus on your breath, you hear the unmistakable sound of your neighbor's lawnmower. You try to ignore it, but it's like trying to meditate at a rock concert.

The Epiphany (Or Lack Thereof... Again)

After much trial and error, you finally have a moment of clarity. You realize that your sacred space might not be perfect, but it's yours. It's a reflection of your journey and your efforts to find peace and balance in a chaotic world. You might not have all the answers, but you're okay with that. After all, life is a lot more fun when you're laughing at the absurdity of it all.

The Moral Of The Story

Creating a sacred space in your home is a personal and meaningful endeavor that promises to bring peace and tranquility to your life. It might not always go according to plan, and there might be some comedic mishaps along the way, but the effort is what counts. So, keep creating, keep laughing, and keep finding your zen in the midst of life's chaos.

ANOTHER QUEST FOR ZEN

A Jovial Guide to Deep Breathing

P racticing deep breathing exercises to calm your mind and connect with your breath sounds like a serene journey into relaxation. But let's face it—trying to achieve a state of zen through deep breathing can be a bit like trying to herd cats during a hurricane. Join us as we embark on a humorous exploration of the quest for deep breathing and the comedic twists and turns that come with it.

The Serenity Seeker

You set out on a quest for inner peace, armed with the knowledge that deep breathing can calm your mind and soothe your soul. You envision yourself sitting cross-legged in a field of wildflowers, breathing deeply and feeling the stress melt away. Little do you know, the universe has some surprises in store for you.

The Breathing Basics

You attempt to practice deep breathing, hoping to find that elusive sense of calm. But just as you start to inhale deeply, you realize that your neighbor has decided to mow their lawn. You try to focus on your breath, but it's like trying to meditate at a rock concert. You wonder if your neighbor is secretly trying to test your patience.

The Mindfulness Mishap

You try to be mindful of your breath, focusing on the rise and fall of your chest with each inhale and exhale. But just as you start to feel a sense of peace, your mind decides to join the conversation with a barrage of random thoughts. You try to silence it, but it's like trying to stop a runaway train with a feather.

The Relaxation Riddle

You attempt to relax into your deep breathing, hoping to feel the tension melt away. But just as you start to feel a sense of calm, your phone decides to chime with a notification. You try to ignore it, but your curiosity gets the better of you. Before you know it, you're scrolling through social media, completely forgetting about your quest for inner peace.

The Epiphany (Or Lack Thereof... Again)

After much trial and error, you finally have a moment of clarity. You realize that deep breathing isn't just about inhaling and exhaling—it's about being present in the moment and embracing whatever comes your way. You might not achieve instant zen, but you're okay with that. After all, life is a lot more fun when you're laughing at the absurdity of it all.

The Moral Of The Story

Practicing deep breathing exercises is a journey that promises to bring calm and clarity to your life. It might not always go according to plan, and there might be some comedic mishaps along the way, but the effort is what counts. So, keep breathing deeply, keep laughing, and keep finding your zen in the midst of life's chaos.

THE MELODIC QUEST

A Comedic Guide to Uplifting Tunes

L istening to uplifting music or chants that elevate your spirit sounds like a soul-stirring experience. But let's face it—finding the perfect song to elevate your mood can be a bit like trying to find a needle in a haystack while wearing mittens. Join us as we embark on a humorous exploration of the quest for uplifting tunes and the comedic twists and turns that come with it.

The Musical Muse

You set out on a quest for the perfect uplifting song, armed with a Spotify playlist and a dream. You envision yourself dancing through fields of daisies, with a soundtrack that lifts your spirits and soothes your soul. Little do you know, the universe has some surprises in store for you.

The Playlist Predicament

You start to curate your uplifting music playlist, carefully selecting songs that promise to elevate your mood. But just as you start to feel the rhythm, your neighbor decides to have a karaoke night. You try to ignore the off-key singing, but it's like trying to meditate at a rock concert.

The Musical Interlude

You attempt to listen to your uplifting tunes, hoping to find that magical song that lifts your spirits. But just as you start to feel a sense of joy, your phone decides to interrupt with a notification. You try to ignore it, but your curiosity gets the better of you. Before you know it, you're scrolling through social media, completely forgetting about your quest for musical bliss.

The Chanting Challenge

You decide to explore the world of chants, hoping to find a spiritual resonance that transcends words. But just as you start to chant, your dog decides to join in with a chorus of barks. You try to maintain your focus, but it's like trying to meditate in a kennel.

The Epiphany (Or Lack Thereof... Again)

After much searching and listening, you finally have a moment of clarity. You realize that uplifting music isn't just about the perfect song—it's about the joy of the journey and the laughter along the way. You might not find the perfect song to elevate your spirit, but you're okay with that. After all, life is a lot more fun when you're laughing at the absurdity of it all.

The Moral Of The Story

Listening to uplifting music or chants is a journey that promises to elevate your spirit and soothe your soul. It might not always go according to plan, and there might be some comedic mishaps along the way, but the joy is in the journey. So, keep listening, keep laughing, and keep searching for that perfect song that lifts your spirits.

THE SELF-CARE SAGA

An Amusing Guide to Nourishing Your Whole Self

P racticing self-care rituals that nourish your body, mind, and soul sounds like a blissful endeavor. But let's face it— trying to achieve a state of zen through self-care can be a bit like trying to juggle flaming torches while riding a unicycle. Join us as we embark on a humorous exploration of the quest for self-care and the comedic twists and turns that come with it.

The Self-Care Symphony Begins

You set out on a mission to practice self-care, armed with scented candles, bath bombs, and a fuzzy robe. You envision yourself luxuriating in a bubble bath, with a cup of herbal tea and a serene expression. Little do you know, the universe has some surprises in store for you.

The Bubble Bath Bungle

You attempt to take a relaxing bubble bath, hoping to wash away the stresses of the day. But just as you start to sink into the warm water, your cat decides to join you. You try to shoo it away, but it's like trying to negotiate with a furry dictator.

The Meditation Mayhem

You try to meditate to clear your mind and nourish your soul. But just as you start to find your inner peace, your stomach decides to join the conversation with an untimely rumble. You try to ignore it, but it's like trying to meditate at a rock concert.

The Yoga Yo-Yo

You attempt to practice yoga to nourish your body and mind. But just as you start to flow through your sun salutations, your dog decides to join in with a series of downward dogs and upward woofs. You try to maintain your focus, but it's like trying to do yoga in a petting zoo.

The Epiphany (Or Lack Thereof... Again)

After much trial and error, you finally have a moment of clarity. You realize that self-care isn't just about the perfect bubble bath or the ideal meditation session—it's about embracing the chaos and finding joy in the journey. You might not achieve instant zen, but you're okay with that. After all, life is a lot more fun when you're laughing at the absurdity of it all.

The Moral Of The Story

Practicing self-care rituals is a journey that promises to nourish your body, mind, and soul. It might not always go according to plan, and there might be some comedic mishaps along the way, but the effort is what counts. So, keep practicing self-care, keep laughing, and keep nourishing your whole self in the midst of life's chaos.

THE CREATIVE COMEDY

A Humorous Guide to Expressing Yourself

Engaging in creative activities that allow you to express your innermost thoughts and feelings sounds like a liberating adventure. But let's face it—trying to unleash your inner artist can be a bit like trying to wrangle a herd of cats into a dance routine. Join us as we embark on a humorous exploration of the quest for creative expression and the comedic twists and turns that come with it.

The Creative Calling

You feel the stirrings of creativity deep within your soul, urging you to pick up a paintbrush, a pen, or a musical instrument. You envision yourself creating a masterpiece that captures the essence of your innermost thoughts and feelings. Little do you know, the universe has some surprises in store for you.

The Artistic Ambition

You attempt to channel your creativity into a work of art, hoping to express yourself in a profound and meaningful way. But just as you start to paint, your cat decides to join in with a series of paw prints that rival Jackson Pollock. You try to incorporate it into your masterpiece, but it's like trying to turn chaos into art.

THE SCENIC ROUTE TO SPIRITUALITY

The Literary Labyrinth

You try your hand at writing, hoping to pen the next great novel that will capture the hearts and minds of readers everywhere. But just as you start to write, your neighbor decides to have a karaoke night. You try to drown out the off-key singing, but it's like trying to write a masterpiece in the middle of a rock concert.

The Musical Mayhem

You attempt to play a musical instrument, hoping to create a symphony that echoes the depths of your soul. But just as you start to play, your dog decides to join in with a series of howls that rival Beethoven's Ninth Symphony. You try to incorporate it into your composition, but it's like trying to conduct an orchestra of chaos.

The Epiphany (Or Lack Thereof... Again)

After much trial and error, you finally have a moment of clarity. You realize that creative expression isn't just about the perfect masterpiece—it's about embracing the process and finding joy in the journey. You might not create a masterpiece that captures the essence of your soul, but you're okay with that. After all, life is a lot more fun when you're laughing at the absurdity of it all.

The Moral Of The Story

Engaging in creative activities is a journey that promises to express your innermost thoughts and feelings. It might not always go according to plan, and there might be some comedic mishaps along the way, but the effort is what counts. So, keep creating, keep laughing, and keep expressing yourself in the midst of life's chaos.

THE COMPASSION COMEDY

*A Hilarious Guide to
Embracing Humanity*

Practicing compassion towards yourself and others, recognizing the shared human experience, sounds like a noble pursuit. But let's face it—trying to be a compassionate human in a world that sometimes feels like a sitcom can be a bit like trying to juggle flaming torches while riding a unicycle on a tightrope. Join us as we embark on a humorous exploration of the quest for compassion and the comedic twists and turns that come with it.

The Compassionate Quest Begins

You set out on a mission to practice compassion, armed with empathy and a smile. You envision yourself as a beacon of kindness, spreading warmth and understanding wherever you go. Little do you know, the universe has some surprises in store for you.

The Self-Compassion Shuffle

You attempt to practice self-compassion, hoping to be kind to yourself in the midst of life's challenges. But just as you start to cut yourself some slack, your inner critic decides to join the conversation with a barrage of self-doubt and criticism. You try to silence it, but it's like trying to reason with a stubborn mule.

The Empathy Expedition

You try to empathize with others, recognizing the shared human experience. But just as you start to understand someone else's perspective, your friend decides to tell a joke that's so bad, it's good. You try to keep a straight face, but it's like trying to hold back a laugh during a serious moment.

The Compassionate Catastrophe

You attempt a grand gesture of compassion, like volunteering at a homeless shelter or organizing a charity event. As you navigate the logistics and details, you realize that compassion is a lot like herding cats—chaotic, unpredictable, and occasionally scratchy. But hey, at least you're making a difference, even if it feels like herding cats.

The Epiphany (Or Lack Thereof... Again)

After much trial and error, you finally have a moment of clarity. You realize that compassion isn't just about being perfect— it's about embracing the messiness of life and finding joy in the journey. You might not achieve instant enlightenment, but you're okay with that. After all, life is a lot more fun when you're laughing at the absurdity of it all.

The Moral Of The Story

Practicing compassion towards yourself and others is a journey that promises to bring warmth and understanding to your life. It might not always go according to plan, and there might be some comedic mishaps along the way, but the effort is what counts. So, keep practicing compassion, keep laughing, and keep embracing the shared human experience in the midst of life's chaos.

THE SPIRITUAL SAFARI

A Lighthearted Guide to
Exploring Traditions

Exploring different spiritual traditions to broaden your understanding of spirituality sounds like a profound adventure. But let's face it—navigating the diverse landscape of beliefs and practices can be a bit like trying to find your way through a maze with a blindfold on. Join us as we embark on a humorous exploration of the quest for spiritual understanding and the comedic twists and turns that come with it.

The Spiritual Safari Begins

You set out on a quest to explore different spiritual traditions, armed with curiosity and an open mind. You envision yourself as a spiritual Indiana Jones, uncovering hidden treasures of wisdom and insight. Little do you know, the universe has some surprises in store for you.

The Tradition Tango

You dive into the world of spiritual traditions, hoping to find one that resonates with your soul. But just as you start to immerse yourself in a new tradition, your friend decides to have a "spiritual awakening" and starts speaking in tongues. You try to keep up, but it's like trying to follow a GPS with a broken compass.

The Belief Buffet

You sample different beliefs and practices, hoping to find the perfect spiritual smorgasbord that satisfies your soul. But just as you start to find your groove, your neighbor decides to start a drum circle at 3 AM. You try to ignore it, but it's like trying to meditate in a construction zone.

The Philosophical Phantasmagoria

You ponder the deep questions of life, like the meaning of existence and the nature of reality. But just as you start to have a profound insight, your cat decides to join the conversation with a series of meows that rival Socrates. You try to maintain your train of thought, but it's like trying to have a deep conversation at a cat convention.

The Epiphany (Or Lack Thereof... Again)

After much exploration and contemplation, you finally have a moment of clarity. You realize that spirituality isn't just about finding the right tradition or belief—it's about embracing the journey and finding joy in the quest for understanding. You might not achieve enlightenment overnight, but you're okay with that. After all, life is a lot more fun when you're laughing at the absurdity of it all.

The Moral Of The Story

Exploring different spiritual traditions is a journey that promises to broaden your understanding of spirituality. It might not always go according to plan, and there might be some comedic mishaps along the way, but the effort is what counts. So, keep exploring, keep laughing, and keep seeking spiritual insight in the midst of life's chaos.

THE VALUES VOYAGE

A Whimsical Guide to
Living in Alignment

Reflecting on your values and how you can live in alignment with them sounds like a soul-searching adventure. But let's face it—trying to live in alignment with your values can be a bit like trying to herd cats during a thunderstorm. Join us as we embark on a humorous exploration of the quest for living in alignment with your values and the comedic twists and turns that come with it.

The Values Voyage Begins

You set sail on a voyage of self-discovery, armed with a compass of your values and a map of your dreams. You envision yourself as a captain of your own destiny, navigating the choppy seas of life with grace and determination. Little do you know, the universe has some surprises in store for you.

The Value Valhalla

You reflect on your values, hoping to gain clarity on what truly matters to you. But just as you start to define your values, your friend decides to have an existential crisis and questions the meaning of life. You try to reassure them, but it's like trying to find a needle in a haystack during a tornado.

The Alignment Avalanche

You attempt to live in alignment with your values, making choices that reflect your deepest beliefs. But just as you start to walk the path of integrity, your dog decides to chase a squirrel and drags you along for the ride. You try to regain your balance, but it's like trying to dance on a tightrope in an earthquake.

The Integrity Interlude

You strive to live with integrity, honoring your values in every action you take. But just as you start to feel like a paragon of virtue, your cat decides to knock over a vase and blame it on the dog. You try to keep a straight face, but it's like trying to keep a secret in a room full of gossips.

The Epiphany (Or Lack Thereof... Again)

After much reflection and laughter, you finally have a moment of clarity. You realize that living in alignment with your values isn't about being perfect—it's about embracing the journey and finding joy in the pursuit of integrity. You might not always get it right, but you're okay with that. After all, life is a lot more fun when you're laughing at the absurdity of it all.

The Moral Of The Story

Reflecting on your values and living in alignment with them is a journey that promises to bring integrity and purpose to your life. It might not always go according to plan, and there might be some comedic mishaps along the way, but the effort is what counts. So, keep reflecting, keep laughing, and keep striving for integrity in the midst of life's chaos.

THE PATIENCE PARADOX

A Jocular Guide to Embracing Imperfection

Practicing patience and acceptance of yourself and others sounds like a noble pursuit. But let's face it—trying to be a paragon of patience in a world that sometimes feels like a circus can be a bit like trying to juggle flaming torches while riding a unicycle on a tightrope. Join us as we embark on a humorous exploration of the quest for patience and the comedic twists and turns that come with it.

The Patience Pilgrimage Begins

You set out on a quest to practice patience, armed with a smile and a deep breath. You envision yourself as a zen master, radiating calm and understanding in the face of chaos. Little do you know, the universe has some surprises in store for you.

The Self-Patience Puzzle

You attempt to practice patience with yourself, hoping to be kind and understanding in the midst of your own shortcomings. But just as you start to cut yourself some slack, your inner critic decides to join the conversation with a barrage of self-doubt and criticism. You try to silence it, but it's like trying to reason with a stubborn mule.

The Patience Paradox

You try to be patient with others, recognizing that everyone has their own journey and struggles. But just as you start to empathize with someone else's situation, your friend decides to tell a joke that's so bad, it's good. You try to keep a straight face, but it's like trying to hold back a laugh during a serious moment.

The Acceptance Avalanche

You strive to accept yourself and others as they are, embracing imperfection and finding beauty in the chaos of life. But just as you start to feel a sense of peace, your cat decides to knock over a vase and blame it on the dog. You try to keep your cool, but it's like trying to stay dry in a rainstorm without an umbrella.

The Epiphany (Or Lack Thereof... Again)

After much reflection and laughter, you finally have a moment of clarity. You realize that practicing patience and acceptance isn't about being perfect—it's about embracing the messiness of life and finding joy in the journey. You might not achieve instant zen, but you're okay with that. After all, life is a lot more fun when you're laughing at the absurdity of it all.

The Moral Of The Story

Practicing patience and acceptance of yourself and others is a journey that promises to bring peace and understanding to your life. It might not always go according to plan, and there might be some comedic mishaps along the way, but the effort is what counts. So, keep practicing, keep laughing, and keep embracing imperfection in the midst of life's chaos.

THE QUIET QUEST

An Entertaining Guide to Inner Silence

Spending time in silence to listen to your inner guidance sounds like a serene endeavor. But let's face it—trying to find inner peace in a world that sometimes feels like a three-ring circus can be a bit like trying to find a needle in a haystack during a tornado. Join us as we embark on a humorous exploration of the quest for inner silence and the comedic twists and turns that come with it.

The Silent Symphony Begins

You set out on a quest for inner silence, armed with a meditation cushion and a determined spirit. You envision yourself as a sage on a mountaintop, attuned to the whispers of the universe. Little do you know, the universe has some surprises in store for you.

The Silence Struggle

You attempt to find inner silence, hoping to quiet the chatter of your mind and connect with your inner guidance. But just as you start to meditate, your neighbor decides to have a karaoke night. You try to drown out the off-key singing, but it's like trying to meditate in a rock concert.

The Inner Dialogue Dilemma

You try to listen to your inner guidance, hoping to find clarity and wisdom. But just as you start to hear a whisper of insight, your stomach decides to join the conversation with an untimely rumble. You try to ignore it, but it's like trying to have a deep conversation at a barbecue.

The Meditation Mayhem

You attempt to meditate in silence, hoping to find peace and tranquility. But just as you start to feel a sense of calm, your dog decides to join in with a series of barks that rival a symphony. You try to maintain your focus, but it's like trying to meditate in a petting zoo.

The Epiphany (Or Lack Thereof... Again)

After much effort and laughter, you finally have a moment of clarity. You realize that inner silence isn't just about the absence of noise—it's about finding peace in the midst of chaos and laughter in the midst of life's absurdity. You might not achieve instant enlightenment, but you're okay with that. After all, life is a lot more fun when you're laughing at the absurdity of it all.

The Moral Of The Story

Spending time in silence to listen to your inner guidance is a journey that promises to bring clarity and wisdom to your life. It might not always go according to plan, and there might be some comedic mishaps along the way, but the effort is what counts. So, keep listening, keep laughing, and keep seeking inner silence in the midst of life's chaos.

THE RITUAL RIDDLE

A Laughable Guide to Meaningful Traditions

E ngaging in rituals that hold personal meaning for you, such as lighting candles or incense, sounds like a soul-stirring experience. But let's face it—trying to find meaning in rituals can be a bit like trying to solve a Rubik's Cube in the dark. Join us as we embark on a humorous exploration of the quest for meaningful rituals and the comedic twists and turns that come with it.

The Ritual Quest Begins

You set out on a quest to engage in meaningful rituals, armed with candles, incense, and a healthy dose of curiosity. You envision yourself as a modern-day mystic, weaving a tapestry of tradition and personal significance. Little do you know, the universe has some surprises in store for you.

The Candle Conundrum

You attempt to light candles as part of your ritual, hoping to create a sense of warmth and tranquility. But just as you strike the match, your cat decides to join in with a series of acrobatic leaps that rival a circus act. You try to keep your cool, but it's like trying to light a candle in a hurricane.

The Incense Interlude

You try to burn incense as part of your ritual, hoping to create an atmosphere of peace and serenity. But just as you light the incense, your smoke alarm decides to join in with a series of beeps that rival a fire drill. You try to fan the smoke away, but it's like trying to clear the air at a barbecue.

The Ritual Riddle

You attempt to find meaning in your rituals, hoping to connect with something deeper and more profound. But just as you start to feel a sense of significance, your neighbor decides to have a drum circle in their backyard. You try to focus, but it's like trying to find a quiet moment in a rock concert.

The Epiphany (Or Lack Thereof... Again)

After much effort and laughter, you finally have a moment of clarity. You realize that meaningful rituals aren't just about the actions themselves—they're about the intention and the journey. You might not achieve instant enlightenment, but you're okay with that. After all, life is a lot more fun when you're laughing at the absurdity of it all.

The Moral Of The Story

Engaging in rituals that hold personal meaning for you is a journey that promises to bring depth and significance to your life. It might not always go according to plan, and there might be some comedic mishaps along the way, but the effort is what counts. So, keep engaging, keep laughing, and keep seeking meaning in the midst of life's chaos.

THE SPIRITUAL SOCIAL

A Jovial Guide to Finding Your Tribe

C onnecting with a spiritual community that shares your beliefs and values sounds like a soulful adventure. But let's face it—trying to find your spiritual tribe in a world that sometimes feels like a sitcom can be a bit like trying to find a needle in a haystack during a tornado. Join us as we embark on a humorous exploration of the quest for a spiritual community and the comedic twists and turns that come with it.

The Spiritual Social Begins

You set out on a quest to find your spiritual tribe, armed with an open heart and a sense of adventure. You envision yourself as a pilgrim, seeking kindred spirits who share your beliefs and values. Little do you know, the universe has some surprises in store for you.

The Community Conundrum

You attempt to find a spiritual community that resonates with you, hoping to find a group of like-minded individuals who understand your journey. But just as you start to feel a sense of belonging, your friend decides to have a "spiritual awakening" and starts speaking in tongues. You try to keep up, but it's like trying to follow a GPS with a broken compass.

The Belief Buffet

You sample different spiritual communities, hoping to find one that feels like home. But just as you start to immerse yourself in a new community, your neighbor decides to start a drum circle at 3 AM. You try to ignore it, but it's like trying to meditate in a construction zone.

The Shared Values Shenanigans

You strive to connect with a community that shares your values, hoping to find a group of people who inspire and uplift you. But just as you start to feel a sense of camaraderie, your dog decides to join in with a series of howls that rival a choir. You try to maintain your focus, but it's like trying to have a serious conversation at a comedy club.

The Epiphany (Or Lack Thereof... Again)

After much searching and laughter, you finally have a moment of clarity. You realize that finding your spiritual tribe isn't just about the perfect community—it's about the joy of the journey and the laughter along the way. You might not find your tribe overnight, but you're okay with that. After all, life is a lot more fun when you're laughing at the absurdity of it all.

The Moral Of The Story

Connecting with a spiritual community that shares your beliefs and values is a journey that promises to bring depth and connection to your life. It might not always go according to plan, and there might be some comedic mishaps along the way, but the effort is what counts. So, keep connecting, keep laughing, and keep seeking your spiritual tribe in the midst of life's chaos.

THE MINDFUL MUNCH

A Mirthful Guide to Eating with Awareness

Practicing mindful eating, savoring each bite and being present with your food, sounds like a deliciously serene endeavor. But let's face it—trying to eat mindfully in a world that sometimes feels like a food fight can be a bit like trying to enjoy a candlelit dinner in the middle of a circus. Join us as we embark on a humorous exploration of the quest for mindful eating and the comedic twists and turns that come with it.

The Mindful Munch Begins

You set out on a quest to practice mindful eating, armed with a fork and a sense of culinary adventure. You envision yourself as a gourmet guru, savoring each bite and finding joy in the simple act of nourishment. Little do you know, the universe has some surprises in store for you.

The Mealtime Marathon

You attempt to eat mindfully, hoping to savor each bite and be present with your food. But just as you start to focus on your meal, your phone decides to chime with a notification. You try to ignore it, but your curiosity gets the better of you. Before you know it, you're scrolling through social media, completely forgetting about your quest for mindful eating.

The Culinary Catastrophe

You try to be present with your food, focusing on the flavors and textures of each bite. But just as you start to appreciate the culinary masterpiece in front of you, your dog decides to join in with a series of barks that rival a food critic. You try to maintain your focus, but it's like trying to enjoy a quiet meal in a dog park.

The Taste Test Tango

You attempt to savor each bite, hoping to experience the full range of flavors in your meal. But just as you start to appreciate the subtle nuances, your cat decides to join in with a series of meows that rival a symphony. You try to keep a straight face, but it's like trying to taste wine at a rock concert.

The Epiphany (Or Lack Thereof... Again)

After much effort and laughter, you finally have a moment of clarity. You realize that practicing mindful eating isn't just about the perfect meal—it's about embracing the chaos and finding joy in the simple act of nourishment. You might not achieve instant culinary enlightenment, but you're okay with that. After all, life is a lot more fun when you're laughing at the absurdity of it all.

The Moral Of The Story

Practicing mindful eating, savoring each bite and being present with your food, is a journey that promises to bring joy and appreciation to your meals. It might not always go according to plan, and there might be some comedic mishaps along the way, but the effort is what counts. So, keep munching mindfully, keep laughing, and keep finding joy in the midst of life's chaos.

THE COSMIC COMEDY

A Hilarious Guide to Interconnectedness

R eflecting on the interconnectedness of all living beings and the universe sounds like a mind-expanding adventure. But let's face it—trying to contemplate the vastness of the cosmos in a world that sometimes feels like a sitcom can be a bit like trying to find your keys in a black hole. Join us as we embark on a humorous exploration of the quest for interconnectedness and the comedic twists and turns that come with it.

The Interconnected Inquiry Begins

You set out on a quest to ponder the interconnectedness of all living beings and the universe, armed with a cosmic curiosity and a healthy dose of existential wonder. You envision yourself as a cosmic explorer, seeking to unravel the mysteries of existence. Little do you know, the universe has some surprises in store for you.

The Universal Uproar

You attempt to contemplate the universe's interconnectedness, hoping to find a sense of unity and belonging. But just as you start to delve into the cosmic web, your neighbor decides to have a karaoke night. You try to ignore the off-key singing, but it's like trying to find inner peace at a rock concert.

The Cosmic Comedy Of Errors

You try to grasp the concept of interconnectedness, imagining the intricate dance of energy and matter that connects all things. But just as you start to feel a sense of cosmic oneness, your cat decides to join in with a series of acrobatic leaps that rival a spacewalk. You try to keep your balance, but it's like trying to find gravity in outer space.

The Interstellar Interruption

You strive to feel connected to all living beings, recognizing the shared experience of existence. But just as you start to feel a sense of cosmic empathy, your dog decides to join in with a series of howls that rival a supernova. You try to maintain your focus, but it's like trying to have a deep conversation at a cosmic carnival.

The Epiphany (Or Lack Thereof... Again)

After much contemplation and laughter, you finally have a moment of cosmic clarity. You realize that pondering interconnectedness isn't just about understanding the universe —it's about embracing the absurdity of existence and finding joy in the journey. You might not achieve cosmic enlightenment, but you're okay with that. After all, life is a lot more fun when you're laughing at the cosmic comedy of it all.

The Moral Of The Story

Reflecting on the interconnectedness of all living beings and the universe is a journey that promises to expand your mind and spark wonder. It might not always go according to plan, and there might be some comedic mishaps along the way, but the effort is what counts. So, keep reflecting, keep laughing, and keep seeking cosmic insight in the midst of life's cosmic comedy.

THE JUDGMENT JIG

A Humorous Guide to Letting Go of Criticism

Practicing non-judgment towards yourself and others sounds like a liberating endeavor. But let's face it—trying to banish judgment in a world that sometimes feels like a judgmental rodeo can be a bit like trying to stop a stampede with a feather. Join us as we embark on a humorous exploration of the quest for non-judgment and the comedic twists and turns that come with it.

The Non-Judgmental Quest Begins

You set out on a quest to practice non-judgment, armed with compassion and a spirit of acceptance. You envision yourself as a zen master, radiating understanding and kindness in the face of criticism. Little do you know, the universe has some surprises in store for you.

The Self-Critique Circus

You attempt to practice non-judgment towards yourself, hoping to be kind and understanding in the face of your own flaws. But just as you start to cut yourself some slack, your inner critic decides to join the conversation with a barrage of self-doubt and criticism. You try to silence it, but it's like trying to reason with a stubborn mule.

The Judgmental Jamboree

You try to practice non-judgment towards others, recognizing that everyone has their own struggles and journeys. But just as you start to empathize with someone else's situation, your friend decides to tell a joke that's so bad, it's good. You try to keep a straight face, but it's like trying to hold back a laugh during a serious moment.

The Compassionate Comedy

You strive to be compassionate towards yourself and others, embracing imperfection and finding beauty in the chaos of life. But just as you start to feel a sense of peace, your dog decides to join in with a series of howls that rival a choir. You try to maintain your composure, but it's like trying to find silence in a symphony.

The Epiphany (Or Lack Thereof... Again)

After much effort and laughter, you finally have a moment of clarity. You realize that practicing non-judgment isn't just about being perfect—it's about embracing the messiness of life and finding joy in the journey. You might not achieve instant enlightenment, but you're okay with that. After all, life is a lot more fun when you're laughing at the absurdity of it all.

The Moral Of The Story

Practicing non-judgment towards yourself and others is a journey that promises to bring compassion and understanding to your life. It might not always go according to plan, and there might be some comedic mishaps along the way, but the effort is what counts. So, keep practicing, keep laughing, and keep embracing imperfection in the midst of life's chaos.

THE CURIOSITY CARNIVAL

A Funny Guide to Embracing Adventure

Cultivating a sense of curiosity and openness to new experiences sounds like a thrilling escapade. But let's face it—trying to stay open-minded in a world that sometimes feels like a carnival can be a bit like trying to navigate a funhouse maze blindfolded. Join us as we embark on a humorous exploration of the quest for curiosity and the comedic twists and turns that come with it.

The Curiosity Quest Begins

You set out on a quest to cultivate curiosity, armed with a sense of adventure and a spirit of openness. You envision yourself as an explorer, ready to discover the wonders of the world around you. Little do you know, the universe has some surprises in store for you.

The Open-Minded Odyssey

You attempt to stay open to new experiences, hoping to embrace the unknown with a sense of wonder. But just as you start to feel adventurous, your friend decides to suggest a "unique" dining experience that involves eating insects. You try to keep an open mind, but it's like trying to swallow a camel in one gulp.

The Adventure Ambush

You try to cultivate a sense of curiosity, seeking out new experiences and knowledge. But just as you start to delve into a new topic, your cat decides to join in with a series of acrobatic leaps that rival a circus act. You try to keep your focus, but it's like trying to read a book in a hurricane.

The Curiosity Carnival

You strive to embrace curiosity as a way of life, finding joy in the pursuit of knowledge and experience. But just as you start to feel a sense of intellectual adventure, your dog decides to join in with a series of howls that rival a symphony. You try to maintain your concentration, but it's like trying to have a deep conversation at a rock concert.

The Epiphany (Or Lack Thereof... Again)

After much exploration and laughter, you finally have a moment of clarity. You realize that cultivating curiosity isn't just about seeking knowledge—it's about embracing the absurdity of life and finding joy in the journey. You might not achieve instant enlightenment, but you're okay with that. After all, life is a lot more fun when you're laughing at the absurdity of it all.

The Moral Of The Story

Cultivating a sense of curiosity and openness to new experiences is a journey that promises to bring excitement and growth to your life. It might not always go according to plan, and there might be some comedic mishaps along the way, but the effort is what counts. So, keep exploring, keep laughing, and keep seeking adventure in the midst of life's carnival.

THE LISTENING CIRCUS

An Amusing Guide to Paying Attention

Practicing deep listening, paying attention to others without judgment or interruption, sounds like a noble pursuit. But let's face it—trying to listen deeply in a world that sometimes feels like a cacophony can be a bit like trying to hear a pin drop in a rock concert. Join us as we embark on a humorous exploration of the quest for deep listening and the comedic twists and turns that come with it.

The Listening Quest Begins

You set out on a quest to practice deep listening, armed with an open heart and a pair of metaphorical earplugs. You envision yourself as a sage, attuned to the subtle nuances of human communication. Little do you know, the universe has some surprises in store for you.

The Interrupting Interlude

You attempt to listen deeply, hoping to give others the space to express themselves fully. But just as you start to focus on the conversation, your friend decides to have a "Eureka!" moment and interrupts with a sudden burst of inspiration. You try to wait patiently, but it's like trying to stop a waterfall with an umbrella.

The Judgment Jamboree

You try to listen without judgment, recognizing that everyone has their own perspective and experiences. But just as you start to empathize with someone else's point of view, your inner critic decides to join the conversation with a barrage of opinions. You try to silence it, but it's like trying to reason with a stubborn mule.

The Empathy Extravaganza

You strive to listen with empathy, seeking to understand the emotions behind the words. But just as you start to connect with the speaker, your cat decides to join in with a series of meows that rival a conversation. You try to maintain your focus, but it's like trying to have a heart-to-heart at a cat convention.

The Epiphany (Or Lack Thereof... Again)

After much effort and laughter, you finally have a moment of clarity. You realize that practicing deep listening isn't just about hearing words—it's about connecting with others on a deeper level and finding joy in the art of communication. You might not achieve instant enlightenment, but you're okay with that. After all, life is a lot more fun when you're laughing at the absurdity of it all.

The Moral Of The Story

Practicing deep listening, paying attention to others without judgment or interruption, is a journey that promises to bring connection and understanding to your relationships. It might not always go according to plan, and there might be some comedic mishaps along the way, but the effort is what counts. So, keep listening, keep laughing, and keep seeking understanding in the midst of life's cacophony.

THE SERVICE SHENANIGANS

A Witty Guide to Selfless Acts

Engaging in acts of service that benefit others without expecting anything in return sounds like a noble endeavor. But let's face it—trying to be selfless in a world that sometimes feels like a sitcom can be a bit like trying to perform a magic trick with a disappearing wand. Join us as we embark on a humorous exploration of the quest for selfless acts and the comedic twists and turns that come with it.

The Service Saga Begins

You set out on a quest to engage in selfless acts of service, armed with kindness and a desire to make the world a better place. You envision yourself as a modern-day superhero, swooping in to save the day without expecting a thank-you note. Little do you know, the universe has some surprises in store for you.

The Altruistic Ambush

You attempt to perform acts of service without expecting anything in return, hoping to make a positive impact on the world. But just as you start to feel like a do-gooder, your friend decides to have a crisis and needs your help. You try to be there for them, but it's like trying to be a superhero with a cape made of spaghetti.

The Selfless Struggle

You try to be selfless in your acts of service, recognizing that true kindness comes from the heart. But just as you start to feel like a beacon of altruism, your cat decides to join in with a series of meows that rival a cry for help. You try to focus, but it's like trying to be a saint in a room full of sinners.

The Kindness Comedy

You strive to perform acts of service with genuine kindness, seeking to make a difference in the lives of others. But just as you start to feel like a philanthropist, your dog decides to join in with a series of howls that rival a charity fundraiser. You try to keep your composure, but it's like trying to be a humanitarian in a dog pound.

The Epiphany (Or Lack Thereof... Again)

After much effort and laughter, you finally have a moment of clarity. You realize that performing selfless acts of service isn't just about the act itself—it's about the intention and the joy of giving without expecting anything in return. You might not achieve instant sainthood, but you're okay with that. After all, life is a lot more fun when you're laughing at the absurdity of it all.

The Moral Of The Story

Engaging in acts of service that benefit others without expecting anything in return is a journey that promises to bring kindness and joy to your life. It might not always go according to plan, and there might be some comedic mishaps along the way, but the effort is what counts. So, keep serving, keep laughing, and keep spreading kindness in the midst of life's comedy.

THE SELF-REFLECTION RODEO

A Comical Guide to Inner Discovery

Practicing self-reflection to gain insight into your thoughts, feelings, and behaviors sounds like a deep dive into the inner workings of the mind. But let's face it—trying to unravel the mysteries of your psyche in a world that sometimes feels like a carnival can be a bit like trying to find a needle in a haystack during a tornado. Join us as we embark on a humorous exploration of the quest for self-reflection and the comedic twists and turns that come with it.

The Self-Reflection Safari Begins

You set out on a quest to practice self-reflection, armed with introspection and a sense of curiosity. You envision yourself as an inner explorer, venturing into the depths of your mind with a metaphorical flashlight. Little do you know, the universe has some surprises in store for you.

The Introspective Interlude

You attempt to reflect on your thoughts, feelings, and behaviors, hoping to gain insight into your inner workings. But just as you start to delve into the depths of your psyche, your phone decides to chime with a notification. You try to ignore it, but your curiosity gets the better of you. Before you know it, you're scrolling through social media, completely forgetting about your quest for self-discovery.

The Emotional Rollercoaster

You try to gain insight into your feelings, seeking to understand the complexities of your emotional landscape. But just as you start to connect with your emotions, your dog decides to join in with a series of howls that rival a dramatic opera. You try to maintain your composure, but it's like trying to have a heart-to-heart at a dog park.

The Behavioral Balancing Act

You strive to analyze your behaviors, hoping to identify patterns and motivations. But just as you start to make progress, your cat decides to join in with a series of acrobatic leaps that rival a circus act. You try to keep your focus, but it's like trying to observe wildlife in a petting zoo.

The Epiphany (Or Lack Thereof... Again)

After much introspection and laughter, you finally have a moment of clarity. You realize that practicing self-reflection isn't just about understanding yourself—it's about embracing the chaos of your mind and finding joy in the journey of self-discovery. You might not achieve instant enlightenment, but you're okay with that. After all, life is a lot more fun when you're laughing at the absurdity of it all.

The Moral Of The Story

Practicing self-reflection to gain insight into your thoughts, feelings, and behaviors is a journey that promises to bring depth and understanding to your life. It might not always go according to plan, and there might be some comedic mishaps along the way, but the effort is what counts. So, keep reflecting, keep laughing, and keep seeking insight in the midst of life's carnival.

THE SOLITARY SOIREE

A Lighthearted Guide to
Reconnecting with Yourself

S pending time in solitude to reconnect with yourself and your inner wisdom sounds like a peaceful escape. But let's face it—trying to find solitude in a world that sometimes feels like a carnival can be a bit like trying to find a quiet corner in a busy theme park. Join us as we embark on a humorous exploration of the quest for solitude and the comedic twists and turns that come with it.

The Solitude Saga Begins

You set out on a quest to spend time in solitude, armed with introspection and a sense of tranquility. You envision yourself as a lone wolf, seeking the wisdom that can only be found in silence. Little do you know, the universe has some surprises in store for you.

The Quest For Quiet

You attempt to find solitude, hoping to escape the noise of the world and reconnect with your inner self. But just as you start to enjoy the peace and quiet, your neighbor decides to start a drum circle in their backyard. You try to drown out the noise, but it's like trying to meditate in the middle of a parade.

THE SCENIC ROUTE TO SPIRITUALITY

The Inner Dialogue Dilemma

You try to reconnect with your inner wisdom, seeking clarity and insight. But just as you start to hear a whisper of wisdom, your stomach decides to join the conversation with an untimely rumble. You try to ignore it, but it's like trying to have a deep conversation at a dinner party.

The Solitary Shenanigans

You strive to find solitude in your thoughts, hoping to tap into your inner wisdom. But just as you start to feel a sense of peace, your dog decides to join in with a series of howls that rival a symphony. You try to maintain your focus, but it's like trying to find silence in a zoo.

The Epiphany (Or Lack Thereof... Again)

After much effort and laughter, you finally have a moment of clarity. You realize that spending time in solitude isn't just about the absence of noise—it's about finding peace in the midst of chaos and laughter in the midst of life's absurdity. You might not achieve instant enlightenment, but you're okay with that. After all, life is a lot more fun when you're laughing at the absurdity of it all.

The Moral Of The Story

Spending time in solitude to reconnect with yourself and your inner wisdom is a journey that promises to bring clarity and peace to your life. It might not always go according to plan, and there might be some comedic mishaps along the way, but the effort is what counts. So, keep seeking solitude, keep laughing, and keep finding peace in the midst of life's carnival.

THE GRATEFUL GAG

A Jocular Guide to Thankfulness

Practicing gratitude for the simple joys in life sounds like a heartwarming endeavor. But let's face it—trying to be thankful in a world that sometimes feels like a comedy sketch can be a bit like trying to find a serious moment in a sitcom. Join us as we embark on a humorous exploration of the quest for gratitude and the comedic twists and turns that come with it.

The Gratitude Gala Begins

You set out on a quest to practice gratitude, armed with appreciation and a sense of wonder. You envision yourself as a grateful guru, finding joy in the little things and spreading positivity like confetti. Little do you know, the universe has some surprises in store for you.

The Thankful Tango

You attempt to practice gratitude for the simple joys in life, hoping to find joy in the everyday moments. But just as you start to feel thankful, your cat decides to join in with a series of meows that rival a choir. You try to keep your focus, but it's like trying to appreciate a sunset during rush hour.

The Appreciation Avalanche

You try to be thankful for the small things, recognizing the beauty in simplicity. But just as you start to feel a sense of appreciation, your dog decides to join in with a series of howls that rival a rock concert. You try to maintain your composure, but it's like trying to find silence in a dog park.

The Grateful Guffaw

You strive to cultivate a spirit of gratitude, seeking to find joy in the mundane. But just as you start to feel thankful, your friend decides to tell a joke that's so bad, it's good. You try to keep a straight face, but it's like trying to hold back a laugh during a serious conversation.

The Epiphany (Or Lack Thereof... Again)

After much effort and laughter, you finally have a moment of clarity. You realize that practicing gratitude isn't just about being thankful—it's about finding joy in the absurdity of life and laughing at the little things. You might not achieve instant enlightenment, but you're okay with that. After all, life is a lot more fun when you're laughing at the absurdity of it all.

The Moral Of The Story

Practicing gratitude for the simple joys in life is a journey that promises to bring joy and appreciation to your life. It might not always go according to plan, and there might be some comedic mishaps along the way, but the effort is what counts. So, keep being thankful, keep laughing, and keep finding joy in the midst of life's comedy.

THE FORGIVENESS FIESTA

A Comedic Guide to Letting Go

Practicing forgiveness towards yourself and others, releasing any lingering resentments, sounds like a liberating endeavor. But let's face it—trying to forgive in a world that sometimes feels like a sitcom can be a bit like trying to find a serious moment in a comedy club. Join us as we embark on a humorous exploration of the quest for forgiveness and the comedic twists and turns that come with it.

The Forgiveness Fandango Begins

You set out on a quest to practice forgiveness, armed with compassion and a desire to let go of the past. You envision yourself as a forgiveness guru, spreading understanding and kindness like confetti. Little do you know, the universe has some surprises in store for you.

The Self-Forgiveness Shuffle

You attempt to practice forgiveness towards yourself, hoping to release any lingering guilt or shame. But just as you start to let go, your inner critic decides to join the conversation with a barrage of self-doubt and criticism. You try to silence it, but it's like trying to reason with a stubborn mule.

The Resentment Rumba

You try to forgive others, recognizing that holding onto resentment only hurts yourself. But just as you start to feel a sense of release, your friend decides to bring up that thing from five years ago. You try to let it go, but it's like trying to deflate a balloon with a pin.

The Forgiveness Fiesta

You strive to cultivate a spirit of forgiveness, seeking to release any negative energy from your life. But just as you start to feel at peace, your dog decides to join in with a series of howls that rival a lamentation. You try to maintain your composure, but it's like trying to find silence in a dog park.

The Epiphany (Or Lack Thereof... Again)

After much effort and laughter, you finally have a moment of clarity. You realize that practicing forgiveness isn't just about letting go—it's about finding humor in the human experience and laughing at life's absurdities. You might not achieve instant enlightenment, but you're okay with that. After all, life is a lot more fun when you're laughing at the absurdity of it all.

The Moral Of The Story

Practicing forgiveness towards yourself and others, releasing any lingering resentments, is a journey that promises to bring peace and freedom to your life. It might not always go according to plan, and there might be some comedic mishaps along the way, but the effort is what counts. So, keep forgiving, keep laughing, and keep finding joy in the midst of life's comedy.

THE JOYFUL JAMBOREE

A Whimsical Guide to Heartwarming Hilarity

Engaging in activities that bring you joy and make your heart sing sounds like a delightful adventure. But let's face it—trying to find joy in a world that sometimes feels like a comedy can be a bit like trying to have a serious conversation at a carnival. Join us as we embark on a humorous exploration of the quest for joy and the comedic twists and turns that come with it.

The Joyful Journey Begins

You set out on a quest to engage in joyful activities, armed with enthusiasm and a desire to embrace the lighter side of life. You envision yourself as a joy-seeking explorer, ready to uncover the hidden treasures of happiness. Little do you know, the universe has some surprises in store for you.

The Pursuit Of Playfulness

You attempt to engage in activities that bring you joy, hoping to rediscover the childlike wonder within you. But just as you start to feel carefree, your phone decides to chime with a barrage of notifications. You try to ignore it, but your curiosity gets the better of you. Before you know it, you're caught in a scrolling frenzy, completely forgetting about your quest for joy.

The Laughter Labyrinth

You try to engage in activities that make your heart sing, seeking out experiences that bring you pure delight. But just as you start to feel the joy bubbling up inside you, your cat decides to join in with a series of acrobatic leaps that rival a circus act. You try to keep your focus, but it's like trying to have a dance party in a tornado.

The Happiness Hurdles

You strive to cultivate a spirit of joy, seeking out activities that uplift your soul. But just as you start to feel a sense of bliss, your dog decides to join in with a series of howls that rival a choir. You try to maintain your composure, but it's like trying to find silence in a zoo.

The Epiphany (Or Lack Thereof... Again)

After much effort and laughter, you finally have a moment of clarity. You realize that pursuing joy isn't just about finding happiness—it's about embracing the chaos of life and finding laughter in the midst of it all. You might not achieve instant enlightenment, but you're okay with that. After all, life is a lot more fun when you're laughing at the absurdity of it all.

The Moral Of The Story

Engaging in activities that bring you joy and make your heart sing is a journey that promises to bring laughter and lightness to your life. It might not always go according to plan, and there might be some comedic mishaps along the way, but the effort is what counts. So, keep seeking joy, keep laughing, and keep finding happiness in the midst of life's comedy.

THE COMPASSIONATE COMEDY

A Hilarious Guide to Self-Love

Practicing self-compassion, treating yourself with kindness and understanding, sounds like a heartwarming endeavor. But let's face it—trying to be kind to yourself in a world that sometimes feels like a comedy can be a bit like trying to find a serious moment in a sitcom. Join us as we embark on a humorous exploration of the quest for self-compassion and the comedic twists and turns that come with it.

The Self-Compassion Saga Begins

You set out on a quest to practice self-compassion, armed with kindness and a desire to treat yourself with gentleness. You envision yourself as a self-love guru, spreading understanding and warmth like confetti. Little do you know, the universe has some surprises in store for you.

The Self-Care Circus

You attempt to practice self-compassion, hoping to treat yourself with the same kindness you offer others. But just as you start to feel at peace, your phone decides to chime with a barrage of notifications. You try to ignore it, but your curiosity gets the better of you. Before you know it, you're caught in a scrolling frenzy, completely forgetting about your quest for self-love.

The Inner Critic Comedy

You try to be kind to yourself, recognizing that self-compassion is the key to inner peace. But just as you start to feel a sense of understanding, your inner critic decides to join the conversation with a barrage of self-doubt and criticism. You try to silence it, but it's like trying to reason with a stubborn mule.

The Self-Kindness Carnival

You strive to cultivate a spirit of self-compassion, seeking to treat yourself with the same care you offer others. But just as you start to feel a sense of warmth, your dog decides to join in with a series of howls that rival a symphony. You try to maintain your composure, but it's like trying to find silence in a dog park.

The Epiphany (Or Lack Thereof... Again)

After much effort and laughter, you finally have a moment of clarity. You realize that practicing self-compassion isn't just about being kind—it's about finding humor in the human experience and laughing at life's absurdities. You might not achieve instant enlightenment, but you're okay with that. After all, life is a lot more fun when you're laughing at the absurdity of it all.

The Moral Of The Story

Practicing self-compassion, treating yourself with kindness and understanding, is a journey that promises to bring peace and warmth to your life. It might not always go according to plan, and there might be some comedic mishaps along the way, but the effort is what counts. So, keep being kind to yourself, keep laughing, and keep finding joy in the midst of life's comedy.

THE HUMOR HANDBOOK

A Playful Guide to Lightening Up

Cultivating a sense of humor and lightness in your approach to life sounds like a barrel of laughs. But let's face it—trying to be lighthearted in a world that sometimes feels like a comedy can be a bit like trying to find a serious moment in a clown convention. Join us as we embark on a humorous exploration of the quest for humor and the comedic twists and turns that come with it.

The Humor Hunt Begins

You set out on a quest to cultivate a sense of humor, armed with wit and a desire to find the funny side of life. You envision yourself as a comedy connoisseur, ready to turn life's challenges into punchlines. Little do you know, the universe has some surprises in store for you.

The Comedy Of Errors

You attempt to cultivate a sense of humor, hoping to find joy in the absurdities of life. But just as you start to see the funny side of things, your phone decides to chime with a barrage of notifications. You try to ignore it, but your curiosity gets the better of you. Before you know it, you're caught in a scrolling frenzy, completely forgetting about your quest for laughter.

The Laughter Labyrinth

You try to see the humor in everyday situations, seeking to find joy in the mundane. But just as you start to chuckle at life's quirks, your cat decides to join in with a series of meows that rival a comedy show. You try to keep your focus, but it's like trying to have a serious conversation at a cat convention.

The Joyful Jester

You strive to be a lighthearted jester, seeking to bring smiles to those around you. But just as you start to crack a joke, your dog decides to join in with a series of howls that rival a stand-up routine. You try to maintain your composure, but it's like trying to perform Shakespeare in a zoo.

The Epiphany (Or Lack Thereof... Again)

After much effort and laughter, you finally have a moment of clarity. You realize that cultivating a sense of humor isn't just about being funny—it's about finding joy in the midst of life's chaos and laughter in the face of adversity. You might not achieve instant comedic genius, but you're okay with that. After all, life is a lot more fun when you're laughing at the absurdity of it all.

The Moral Of The Story

Cultivating a sense of humor and lightness in your approach to life is a journey that promises to bring laughter and joy to your life. It might not always go according to plan, and there might be some comedic mishaps along the way, but the effort is what counts. So, keep laughing, keep smiling, and keep finding joy in the midst of life's comedy.

THE KINDNESS COMEDY

A Zany Guide to Compassion

Practicing loving-kindness meditation to cultivate feelings of compassion towards yourself and others sounds like a heartwarming endeavor. But let's face it—trying to be compassionate in a world that sometimes feels like a comedy can be a bit like trying to have a serious conversation at a clown convention. Join us as we embark on a humorous exploration of the quest for compassion and the comedic twists and turns that come with it.

The Compassion Crusade Begins

You set out on a quest to practice loving-kindness meditation, armed with empathy and a desire to spread warmth and understanding. You envision yourself as a compassion champion, ready to shower the world with kindness like confetti. Little do you know, the universe has some surprises in store for you.

The Meditation Mishap

You attempt to practice loving-kindness meditation, hoping to cultivate feelings of compassion. But just as you start to feel the warmth spreading through you, your phone decides to chime with a barrage of notifications. You try to ignore it, but your curiosity gets the better of you. Before you know it, you're caught in a scrolling frenzy, completely forgetting about your quest for kindness.

The Self-Compassion Circus

You try to cultivate feelings of compassion towards yourself, recognizing that self-love is the key to spreading kindness. But just as you start to feel a sense of warmth, your inner critic decides to join the conversation with a barrage of self-doubt and criticism. You try to silence it, but it's like trying to reason with a stubborn mule.

The Empathy Extravaganza

You strive to cultivate feelings of compassion towards others, seeking to spread warmth and understanding. But just as you start to feel a sense of empathy, your dog decides to join in with a series of howls that rival a symphony. You try to maintain your composure, but it's like trying to find silence in a zoo.

The Epiphany (Or Lack Thereof... Again)

After much effort and laughter, you finally have a moment of clarity. You realize that practicing loving-kindness meditation isn't just about being kind—it's about finding humor in the human experience and laughing at life's absurdities. You might not achieve instant enlightenment, but you're okay with that. After all, life is a lot more fun when you're laughing at the absurdity of it all.

The Moral Of The Story

Practicing loving-kindness meditation to cultivate feelings of compassion towards yourself and others is a journey that promises to bring warmth and understanding to your life. It might not always go according to plan, and there might be some comedic mishaps along the way, but the effort is what counts. So, keep spreading kindness, keep laughing, and keep finding joy in the midst of life's comedy.

THE IMPERMANENT IMPROVISATION

A Mirthful Guide to Embracing the Present

Reflecting on the impermanence of life and the importance of living in the present moment sounds like a deep dive into existentialism. But let's face it—trying to contemplate the meaning of life in a world that sometimes feels like a comedy can be a bit like trying to have a serious conversation at a carnival. Join us as we embark on a humorous exploration of the quest for mindfulness and the comedic twists and turns that come with it.

The Mindful Misadventure Begins

You set out on a quest to reflect on the impermanence of life, armed with introspection and a desire to embrace the present moment. You envision yourself as a philosophical ponderer, ready to uncover the mysteries of existence. Little do you know, the universe has some surprises in store for you.

The Transient Tango

You attempt to reflect on the impermanence of life, hoping to find wisdom in the ebb and flow of existence. But just as you start to contemplate the fleeting nature of time, your phone decides to chime with a barrage of notifications. You try to ignore it, but your curiosity gets the better of you. Before you know it, you're caught in a scrolling frenzy, completely forgetting about your quest for mindfulness.

The Present Moment Play

You try to embrace the present moment, seeking to find joy in the here and now. But just as you start to feel a sense of presence, your cat decides to join in with a series of meows that rival a conversation. You try to maintain your focus, but it's like trying to meditate in a zoo.

The Zen Zinger

You strive to live in the present moment, recognizing that now is all there is. But just as you start to feel a sense of peace, your dog decides to join in with a series of howls that rival a meditation chant. You try to maintain your composure, but it's like trying to find silence in a dog park.

The Epiphany (Or Lack Thereof... Again)

After much effort and laughter, you finally have a moment of clarity. You realize that reflecting on the impermanence of life isn't just about deep thoughts—it's about finding humor in the human experience and laughing at life's absurdities. You might not achieve instant enlightenment, but you're okay with that. After all, life is a lot more fun when you're laughing at the absurdity of it all.

The Moral Of The Story

Reflecting on the impermanence of life and the importance of

living in the present moment is a journey that promises to bring clarity and peace to your life. It might not always go according to plan, and there might be some comedic mishaps along the way, but the effort is what counts. So, keep reflecting, keep laughing, and keep finding joy in the midst of life's comedy.

THE MINDFUL MARCH

An Entertaining Guide to
Walking with Awareness

Practicing mindfulness walking, paying attention to each step and the sensations in your body, sounds like a peaceful stroll through the park. But let's face it—trying to be mindful in a world that sometimes feels like a comedy can be a bit like trying to find a quiet moment in a marching band. Join us as we embark on a humorous exploration of the quest for mindful walking and the comedic twists and turns that come with it.

The Mindful Meander Begins

You set out on a quest to practice mindfulness walking, armed with awareness and a desire to connect with the present moment. You envision yourself as a mindful wanderer, ready to tread lightly and notice the world around you. Little do you know, the universe has some surprises in store for you.

The Conscious Commotion

You attempt to practice mindfulness walking, hoping to be fully present with each step. But just as you start to feel the rhythm of your walk, your phone decides to chime with a barrage of notifications. You try to ignore it, but your curiosity gets the better of you. Before you know it, you're caught in a scrolling frenzy, completely forgetting about your quest for mindfulness.

The Sensory Stroll

You try to pay attention to the sensations in your body as you walk, seeking to be fully aware of each movement. But just as you start to feel grounded in your body, your dog decides to join in with a series of howls that rival a nature soundtrack. You try to maintain your focus, but it's like trying to meditate in a dog park.

The Mindful Mosey

You strive to be mindful of each step, recognizing the beauty in the simple act of walking. But just as you start to feel a sense of peace, your friend decides to join you with a series of jokes that rival a comedy show. You try to keep your composure, but it's like trying to walk a tightrope in a circus.

The Epiphany (Or Lack Thereof... Again)

After much effort and laughter, you finally have a moment of clarity. You realize that practicing mindfulness walking isn't just about being present—it's about finding humor in the human experience and laughing at life's absurdities. You might not achieve instant enlightenment, but you're okay with that. After all, life is a lot more fun when you're laughing at the absurdity of it all.

The Moral Of The Story

Practicing mindfulness walking, paying attention to each step and the sensations in your body, is a journey that promises to bring awareness and presence to your life. It might not always go according to plan, and there might be some comedic mishaps along the way, but the effort is what counts. So, keep walking, keep laughing, and keep finding joy in the midst of life's comedy.

THE WELLNESS WACKINESS

A Laughable Guide to
Fitness and Nutrition

E ngaging in practices that promote physical well-being, such as exercise and healthy eating, sounds like a recipe for health and happiness. But let's face it—trying to stay fit and eat well in a world that sometimes feels like a comedy can be a bit like trying to have a serious conversation at a food festival. Join us as we embark on a humorous exploration of the quest for wellness and the comedic twists and turns that come with it.

The Fitness Fiasco Begins

You set out on a quest to engage in practices that promote physical well-being, armed with determination and a desire to be healthy. You envision yourself as a wellness warrior, ready to conquer fitness and nutrition challenges with gusto. Little do you know, the universe has some surprises in store for you.

The Exercise Expedition

You attempt to engage in regular exercise, hoping to stay fit and healthy. But just as you start to feel the burn, your phone decides to chime with a barrage of notifications. You try to ignore it, but your curiosity gets the better of you. Before you know it, you're caught in a scrolling frenzy, completely forgetting about your quest for fitness.

The Nutritional Nonsense

You try to eat a balanced diet, seeking to nourish your body with healthy foods. But just as you start to enjoy a nutritious meal, your cat decides to join in with a series of meows that rival a dinner conversation. You try to maintain your focus, but it's like trying to have a serious discussion at a cat café.

The Wellness Whirlwind

You strive to maintain a healthy lifestyle, recognizing the importance of physical well-being. But just as you start to feel a sense of accomplishment, your dog decides to join in with a series of howls that rival a workout playlist. You try to keep your composure, but it's like trying to do yoga in a dog park.

The Epiphany (Or Lack Thereof... Again)

After much effort and laughter, you finally have a moment of clarity. You realize that engaging in practices that promote physical well-being isn't just about being healthy—it's about finding humor in the human experience and laughing at life's absurdities. You might not achieve instant fitness guru status, but you're okay with that. After all, life is a lot more fun when you're laughing at the absurdity of it all.

The Moral Of The Story

Engaging in practices that promote physical well-being, such as exercise and healthy eating, is a journey that promises to bring health and vitality to your life. It might not always go according to plan, and there might be some comedic mishaps along the way, but the effort is what counts. So, keep moving, keep eating well, and keep finding joy in the midst of life's comedy.

THE FORGIVENESS FROLIC

A Jovial Guide to Letting Go of the Past

Practicing forgiveness towards yourself for any past mistakes or shortcomings sounds like a liberating endeavor. But let's face it—trying to forgive yourself in a world that sometimes feels like a comedy can be a bit like trying to find a serious moment in a sitcom. Join us as we embark on a humorous exploration of the quest for self-forgiveness and the comedic twists and turns that come with it.

The Self-Forgiveness Saga Begins

You set out on a quest to practice forgiveness towards yourself, armed with compassion and a desire to let go of the past. You envision yourself as a self-forgiveness guru, ready to release any lingering guilt or shame. Little do you know, the universe has some surprises in store for you.

The Forgiveness Frolic

You attempt to practice self-forgiveness, hoping to release any negative energy from your life. But just as you start to feel at peace, your phone decides to chime with a barrage of notifications. You try to ignore it, but your curiosity gets the better of you. Before you know it, you're caught in a scrolling frenzy, completely forgetting about your quest for forgiveness.

The Forgiveness Frolic

You try to forgive yourself for past mistakes, recognizing that self-compassion is the key to moving forward. But just as you start to let go, your inner critic decides to join the conversation with a barrage of self-doubt and criticism. You try to silence it, but it's like trying to reason with a stubborn mule.

The Forgiveness Fandango

You strive to cultivate a spirit of self-forgiveness, seeking to let go of any lingering regrets. But just as you start to feel a sense of release, your dog decides to join in with a series of howls that rival a lamentation. You try to maintain your composure, but it's like trying to find silence in a dog park.

The Epiphany (Or Lack Thereof... Again)

After much effort and laughter, you finally have a moment of clarity. You realize that practicing forgiveness towards yourself isn't just about letting go—it's about finding humor in the human experience and laughing at life's absurdities. You might not achieve instant enlightenment, but you're okay with that. After all, life is a lot more fun when you're laughing at the absurdity of it all.

The Moral Of The Story

Practicing forgiveness towards yourself for any past mistakes or shortcomings is a journey that promises to bring peace and freedom to your life. It might not always go according to plan, and there might be some comedic mishaps along the way, but the effort is what counts. So, keep forgiving, keep laughing, and keep finding joy in the midst of life's comedy.

THE INTERCONNECTED INTERLUDE

A Humorous Guide to Cosmic Connections

Reflecting on the interconnectedness of all things and your place in the web of life sounds like a cosmic contemplation. But let's face it—trying to ponder the universe in a world that sometimes feels like a comedy can be a bit like trying to have a serious conversation at a cosmic carnival. Join us as we embark on a humorous exploration of the quest for cosmic connection and the comedic twists and turns that come with it.

The Cosmic Contemplation Commences

You set out on a quest to reflect on the interconnectedness of all things, armed with introspection and a desire to understand your place in the universe. You envision yourself as a cosmic explorer, ready to unravel the mysteries of existence. Little do you know, the universe has some surprises in store for you.

The Interconnected Inquisition

You attempt to reflect on the interconnectedness of all things, hoping to find wisdom in the cosmic dance of life. But just as you start to feel the cosmic energy flowing through you, your phone decides to chime with a barrage of notifications. You try to ignore it, but your curiosity gets the better of you. Before you know it, you're caught in a scrolling frenzy, completely forgetting about your quest for cosmic insight.

The Web Of Wonder

You try to contemplate your place in the web of life, seeking to find meaning in the grand tapestry of existence. But just as you start to feel a sense of connection, your cat decides to join in with a series of meows that rival a cosmic choir. You try to maintain your focus, but it's like trying to meditate in a cat café.

The Universal Unraveling

You strive to understand the interconnectedness of all things, recognizing the beauty of cosmic harmony. But just as you start to feel a sense of unity, your dog decides to join in with a series of howls that rival a celestial symphony. You try to keep your composure, but it's like trying to find silence in a starry night.

The Epiphany (Or Lack Thereof... Again)

After much effort and laughter, you finally have a moment of clarity. You realize that reflecting on the interconnectedness of all things isn't just about cosmic wisdom—it's about finding humor in the human experience and laughing at life's absurdities. You might not achieve instant enlightenment, but you're okay with that. After all, life is a lot more fun when you're laughing at the absurdity of it all.

The Moral Of The Story

Reflecting on the interconnectedness of all things and your

place in the web of life is a journey that promises to bring insight and wonder to your life. It might not always go according to plan, and there might be some comedic mishaps along the way, but the effort is what counts. So, keep reflecting, keep laughing, and keep finding joy in the midst of life's cosmic comedy.

THE GRATITUDE GALA

A Funny Guide to Counting Your Blessings

Practicing gratitude for the abundance in your life, both material and spiritual, sounds like a heartwarming celebration. But let's face it—trying to be grateful in a world that sometimes feels like a comedy can be a bit like trying to have a serious conversation at a gratitude gala. Join us as we embark on a humorous exploration of the quest for gratitude and the comedic twists and turns that come with it.

The Gratitude Gathering Begins

You set out on a quest to practice gratitude for the abundance in your life, armed with appreciation and a desire to count your blessings. You envision yourself as a gratitude guru, ready to shower the world with thankfulness like confetti. Little do you know, the universe has some surprises in store for you.

The Grateful Gaffe

You attempt to practice gratitude, hoping to cultivate a spirit of thankfulness. But just as you start to feel the warmth of gratitude, your phone decides to chime with a barrage of notifications. You try to ignore it, but your curiosity gets the better of you. Before you know it, you're caught in a scrolling

THE SCENIC ROUTE TO SPIRITUALITY

frenzy, completely forgetting about your quest for appreciation.

The Abundance Amusement

You try to be grateful for the abundance in your life, recognizing the richness of your experiences. But just as you start to feel a sense of abundance, your cat decides to join in with a series of meows that rival a gratitude meditation. You try to maintain your focus, but it's like trying to have a peaceful moment in a cat café.

The Spiritual Serenade

You strive to be grateful for the spiritual abundance in your life, seeking to appreciate the intangible blessings. But just as you start to feel a sense of spiritual connection, your dog decides to join in with a series of howls that rival a spiritual chant. You try to keep your composure, but it's like trying to meditate in a dog park.

The Epiphany (Or Lack Thereof... Again)

After much effort and laughter, you finally have a moment of clarity. You realize that practicing gratitude for the abundance in your life isn't just about being thankful—it's about finding humor in the human experience and laughing at life's absurdities. You might not achieve instant enlightenment, but you're okay with that. After all, life is a lot more fun when you're laughing at the absurdity of it all.

The Moral Of The Story

Practicing gratitude for the abundance in your life, both material and spiritual, is a journey that promises to bring joy and appreciation to your life. It might not always go according to plan, and there might be some comedic mishaps along the way, but the effort is what counts. So, keep counting your blessings, keep laughing, and keep finding joy in the midst of life's gratitude gala.

THE CREATIVITY CARNIVAL

An Amusing Guide to Unleashing Your Imagination

Engaging in activities that nurture your creativity and allow you to express yourself sounds like a vibrant artistic adventure. But let's face it—trying to be creative in a world that sometimes feels like a comedy can be a bit like trying to have a serious conversation at an art gallery opening. Join us as we embark on a humorous exploration of the quest for creativity and the comedic twists and turns that come with it.

The Creative Quest Commences

You set out on a quest to engage in activities that nurture your creativity, armed with imagination and a desire to express yourself. You envision yourself as a creative wizard, ready to weave artistic spells and unleash your inner muse. Little do you know, the universe has some surprises in store for you.

The Artistic Ambush

You attempt to engage in creative activities, hoping to let your imagination run wild. But just as you start to feel the creative juices flowing, your phone decides to chime with a barrage of notifications. You try to ignore it, but your curiosity gets the better of you. Before you know it, you're caught in a scrolling frenzy, completely forgetting about your quest for creativity.

The Expressive Extravaganza

You try to express yourself through art, seeking to unleash your inner artist. But just as you start to get into the flow, your cat decides to join in with a series of meows that rival a creative brainstorm. You try to maintain your focus, but it's like trying to paint a masterpiece in a cat café.

The Imagination Indulgence

You strive to nurture your creativity, recognizing the importance of artistic expression. But just as you start to feel a sense of inspiration, your dog decides to join in with a series of howls that rival a symphony. You try to keep your composure, but it's like trying to compose a sonnet in a dog park.

The Epiphany (Or Lack Thereof... Again)

After much effort and laughter, you finally have a moment of clarity. You realize that engaging in activities that nurture your creativity isn't just about being artistic—it's about finding humor in the human experience and laughing at life's absurdities. You might not achieve instant creative genius, but you're okay with that. After all, life is a lot more fun when you're laughing at the absurdity of it all.

The Moral Of The Story

Engaging in activities that nurture your creativity and allow you to express yourself is a journey that promises to bring joy and inspiration to your life. It might not always go according to plan, and there might be some comedic mishaps along the way, but the effort is what counts. So, keep creating, keep laughing, and keep finding joy in the midst of life's creative carnival.

THE ACCEPTANCE ADVENTURE

A Witty Guide to Embracing Uniqueness

Practicing acceptance of yourself and others, recognizing that everyone is on their own unique journey, sounds like a liberating quest. But let's face it—trying to be accepting in a world that sometimes feels like a comedy can be a bit like trying to have a serious conversation at a costume party. Join us as we embark on a humorous exploration of the quest for acceptance and the comedic twists and turns that come with it.

The Acceptance Expedition Begins

You set out on a quest to practice acceptance, armed with understanding and a desire to embrace diversity. You envision yourself as an acceptance ambassador, ready to celebrate uniqueness and foster inclusivity. Little do you know, the universe has some surprises in store for you.

The Diversity Dilemma

You attempt to practice acceptance, hoping to embrace the differences in others. But just as you start to feel a sense of openness, your phone decides to chime with a barrage of notifications. You try to ignore it, but your curiosity gets the better of you. Before you know it, you're caught in a scrolling frenzy, completely forgetting about your quest for acceptance.

The Uniqueness Uproar

You try to accept yourself as you are, recognizing that you are a unique individual. But just as you start to feel comfortable in your own skin, your cat decides to join in with a series of meows that rival a personal pep talk. You try to maintain your confidence, but it's like trying to boost your self-esteem in a cat café.

The Inclusivity Invasion

You strive to be accepting of others, recognizing the beauty of diversity. But just as you start to feel a sense of unity, your dog decides to join in with a series of howls that rival a community choir. You try to keep your composure, but it's like trying to build a sense of belonging in a dog park.

The Epiphany (Or Lack Thereof... Again)

After much effort and laughter, you finally have a moment of clarity. You realize that practicing acceptance of yourself and others isn't just about being open-minded—it's about finding humor in the human experience and laughing at life's absurdities. You might not achieve instant enlightenment, but you're okay with that. After all, life is a lot more fun when you're laughing at the absurdity of it all.

The Moral Of The Story

Practicing acceptance of yourself and others, recognizing that everyone is on their own unique journey, is a journey that promises to bring understanding and compassion to your life. It might not always go according to plan, and there might be some comedic mishaps along the way, but the effort is what counts. So, keep accepting, keep laughing, and keep finding joy in the midst of life's acceptance adventure.

THE ADMIRATION AMUSEMENT

A Hilarious Guide to Emulating Excellence

Reflecting on the qualities you admire in others and how you can cultivate them in yourself sounds like a thoughtful introspection. But let's face it—trying to emulate greatness in a world that sometimes feels like a comedy can be a bit like trying to have a serious conversation at a talent show. Join us as we embark on a humorous exploration of the quest for self-improvement and the comedic twists and turns that come with it.

The Admiration Adventure Begins

You set out on a quest to reflect on the qualities you admire in others, armed with inspiration and a desire to grow. You envision yourself as a self-improvement guru, ready to transform into the best version of yourself. Little do you know, the universe has some surprises in store for you.

The Excellence Examination

You attempt to reflect on the qualities you admire in others, hoping to learn from their example. But just as you start to feel inspired, your phone decides to chime with a barrage of notifications. You try to ignore it, but your curiosity gets the better of you. Before you know it, you're caught in a scrolling frenzy, completely forgetting about your quest for self-improvement.

The Self-Improvement Spectacle

You try to cultivate the qualities you admire in others, recognizing the potential for growth within yourself. But just as you start to envision your transformation, your cat decides to join in with a series of meows that rival a motivational speech. You try to maintain your focus, but it's like trying to find motivation in a cat café.

The Personal Growth Parade

You strive to emulate the greatness you admire in others, seeking to embody their positive qualities. But just as you start to feel a sense of empowerment, your dog decides to join in with a series of howls that rival a motivational seminar. You try to keep your composure, but it's like trying to find inspiration in a dog park.

The Epiphany (Or Lack Thereof... Again)

After much effort and laughter, you finally have a moment of clarity. You realize that reflecting on the qualities you admire in others and how you can cultivate them in yourself isn't just about personal growth—it's about finding humor in the human experience and laughing at life's absurdities. You might not achieve instant transformation, but you're okay with that. After all, life is a lot more fun when you're laughing at the absurdity of it all.

The Moral Of The Story

Reflecting on the qualities you admire in others and how you can cultivate them in yourself is a journey that promises to bring growth and self-awareness to your life. It might not always go according to plan, and there might be some comedic mishaps along the way, but the effort is what counts. So, keep reflecting, keep laughing, and keep finding joy in the midst of life's self-improvement spectacle.

THE ROAD TO FOCUSVILLE

A Comical Expedition in
Attention Management

Welcome to the Road to Focusville, where we'll embark on a humorous journey through the practice of staying focused on the road. Get ready for a hilarious road trip of attention management and distraction detours as we navigate the highway of concentration with a honk and a wink to the distractions along the way.

The Road To Focusville Departure

You buckle up for the journey of staying focused, armed with a roadmap of mindfulness and a GPS of concentration. You envision yourself as a driver of attention, ready to navigate the twists and turns of distraction with sharp reflexes and a sense of humor. But as soon as you hit the road, your mind starts to wander like a lost tourist in a foreign city.

The Road To Focusville Detour

You attempt to practice staying focused on the road, hoping to maintain your attention despite the allure of distractions. But just as you start to concentrate, a billboard catches your eye —a giant sign advertising the world's largest rubber band ball, tempting you to take the next exit like a child in a candy store.

You try to resist, but it's like trying to ignore a parade of dancing elephants.

The Road To Focusville Dilemma

You try to stay focused on the road, recognizing the importance of attention management. But just as you start to concentrate, a song comes on the radio—a catchy tune that gets stuck in your head, playing on repeat like a broken record. You try to change the station, but it's like trying to unhear a catchy jingle.

The Road To Focusville Distraction

You strive to stay focused on the road, understanding that distractions can lead to accidents. But just as you start to focus, a squirrel darts across the road—a furry menace that demands your attention like a traffic cop with a ticket book. You try to stay on course, but it's like trying to dodge raindrops in a thunderstorm.

The Road To Focusville Destination

After much effort and laughter, you finally reach your destination of focus. You realize that practicing staying focused on the road isn't just about avoiding distractions—it's about finding humor in the journey and laughing at the absurdity of it all. You might not achieve perfect concentration, but you're okay with that. After all, life is a lot more fun when you're laughing at the Road to Focusville of it all.

The Moral Of The Story

Practicing staying focused on the road is a journey that promises to bring mindfulness and attention management. It might not always go according to plan, and there might be some comedic mishaps along the way, but the effort is what counts. So, keep driving, keep laughing, and keep finding joy in the midst of life's Road to Focusville.

THE CLARITY COMEDY

A Lighthearted Guide to Mental Zen

Engaging in practices that promote mental clarity and focus, such as meditation and deep breathing, sounds like a journey to inner peace. But let's face it—trying to find mental zen in a world that sometimes feels like a comedy can be a bit like trying to have a serious conversation at a clown convention. Join us as we embark on a humorous exploration of the quest for mental clarity and the comedic twists and turns that come with it.

The Mental Clarity Mission Begins

You set out on a quest to engage in practices that promote mental clarity and focus, armed with determination and a desire for inner peace. You envision yourself as a mental zen master, ready to silence the chaos of the mind and find clarity amidst the madness. Little do you know, the universe has some surprises in store for you.

The Clarity Chaos

You attempt to practice meditation, hoping to quiet the mind and find inner stillness. But just as you start to feel the peace within, your phone decides to chime with a barrage of notifications. You try to ignore it, but your curiosity gets the better of you. Before you know it, you're caught in a scrolling frenzy, completely forgetting about your quest for mental clarity.

The Focus Fiasco

You try to focus on your breath, seeking to cultivate a sense of calm and presence. But just as you start to feel centered, your cat decides to join in with a series of meows that rival a meditation chant. You try to maintain your focus, but it's like trying to find stillness in a cat café.

The Zen Zinger

You strive to find mental clarity amidst the chaos, recognizing the importance of inner peace. But just as you start to feel a sense of clarity, your dog decides to join in with a series of howls that rival a meditation mantra. You try to keep your composure, but it's like trying to find tranquility in a dog park.

The Epiphany (Or Lack Thereof... Again)

After much effort and laughter, you finally have a moment of clarity. You realize that engaging in practices that promote mental clarity and focus isn't just about finding peace—it's about finding humor in the human experience and laughing at life's absurdities. You might not achieve instant zen master status, but you're okay with that. After all, life is a lot more fun when you're laughing at the absurdity of it all.

The Moral Of The Story

Engaging in practices that promote mental clarity and focus, such as meditation and deep breathing, is a journey that promises to bring peace and clarity to your mind. It might not always go according to plan, and there might be some comedic mishaps along the way, but the effort is what counts. So, keep practicing, keep laughing, and keep finding joy in the midst of life's mental clarity comedy.

THE GRATITUDE GAMBOL

A Jocular Guide to
Embracing Challenges

Practicing gratitude for the challenges in your life, recognizing them as opportunities for growth, sounds like a noble endeavor. But let's face it—trying to be grateful for challenges in a world that sometimes feels like a comedy can be a bit like trying to have a serious conversation at a clown convention. Join us as we embark on a humorous exploration of the quest for gratitude amidst challenges and the comedic twists and turns that come with it.

The Gratitude Gamble Begins

You set out on a quest to practice gratitude for the challenges in your life, armed with resilience and a desire for personal growth. You envision yourself as a gratitude guru, ready to turn obstacles into stepping stones. Little do you know, the universe has some surprises in store for you.

The Challenge Circus

You attempt to practice gratitude for the challenges you face, hoping to see them as opportunities for growth. But just as you start to feel the gratitude flowing, your phone decides to chime with a barrage of notifications. You try to ignore it, but your curiosity gets the better of you. Before you know it, you're caught in a scrolling frenzy, completely forgetting about your quest for gratitude.

The Growth Guffaw

You try to be grateful for the challenges that come your way, recognizing the lessons they can teach. But just as you start to appreciate the silver linings, your cat decides to join in with a series of meows that rival a motivational speech. You try to maintain your focus, but it's like trying to find wisdom in a cat café.

The Opportunity Opera

You strive to see challenges as opportunities for growth, seeking to embrace them with gratitude. But just as you start to feel a sense of empowerment, your dog decides to join in with a series of howls that rival a motivational seminar. You try to keep your composure, but it's like trying to find inspiration in a dog park.

The Epiphany (Or Lack Thereof... Again)

After much effort and laughter, you finally have a moment of clarity. You realize that practicing gratitude for the challenges in your life isn't just about personal growth—it's about finding humor in the human experience and laughing at life's absurdities. You might not achieve instant enlightenment, but you're okay with that. After all, life is a lot more fun when you're laughing at the absurdity of it all.

The Moral Of The Story

Practicing gratitude for the challenges in your life, recognizing

them as opportunities for growth, is a journey that promises to bring resilience and wisdom to your life. It might not always go according to plan, and there might be some comedic mishaps along the way, but the effort is what counts. So, keep being grateful, keep laughing, and keep finding joy in the midst of life's gratitude gambol.

THE IMPACT INVESTIGATION

A Droll Quest for Understanding

Welcome to the Impact Investigation, where we'll embark on a humorous journey through the reflection on the impact of your actions on others. Get ready for a detective story full of twists, turns, and comedic mishaps as we uncover the mysteries of human interaction with a magnifying glass of introspection and a notepad of nonsense.

The Impact Investigation Interrogation

You don your detective hat of introspection, armed with a notepad of nonsense and a magnifying glass of mindfulness. You envision yourself as a sleuth of social dynamics, ready to unravel the complexities of your influence with wit and insight. But as soon as you start to investigate, your thoughts scatter like suspects in a crowded room.

The Impact Investigation Interference

You attempt to reflect on the impact of your actions on others, hoping to gain insight into your role in their lives. But just as you start to connect the dots, a distraction appears—a squirrel outside your window doing acrobatics like a circus performer on caffeine. You try to refocus, but it's like trying to solve a mystery in a house of mirrors.

The Impact Investigation Interruption

You try to reflect on the impact of your actions, recognizing the importance of empathy and understanding. But just as you start to empathize, your phone buzzes with a notification, tempting you to check your messages like a cat with a laser pointer. You try to resist, but it's like trying to ignore a ringing phone in a quiet library.

The Impact Investigation Impersonation

You strive to reflect on the impact of your actions, understanding that every choice has a consequence. But just as you start to ponder, your mind plays tricks on you— suddenly, you're imagining yourself as a character in a detective novel, solving crimes of kindness and misdemeanors of misunderstanding. You try to shake off the fantasy, but it's like trying to catch a shadow with your bare hands.

The Impact Investigation Insight

After much effort and laughter, you finally have a moment of insight. You realize that reflecting on the impact of your actions on others isn't just about understanding consequences —it's about finding humor in the unpredictability of human interaction and laughing at the absurdity of it all. You might not solve the case of social dynamics, but you're okay with that. After all, life is a lot more fun when you're laughing at the Impact Investigation of it all.

The Moral Of The Story

Reflecting on the impact of your actions on others is a journey that promises to bring insight and empathy. It might not always go according to plan, and there might be some comedic mishaps along the way, but the effort is what counts. So, keep investigating, keep laughing, and keep finding joy in the midst of life's Impact Investigation.

THE MINDFUL MELODRAMA

A Whimsical Guide to Listening

Practicing mindfulness listening, giving your full attention to the speaker without interrupting, sounds like a noble endeavor. But let's face it—trying to be mindful in a world that sometimes feels like a comedy can be a bit like trying to have a serious conversation at a comedy club. Join us as we embark on a humorous exploration of the quest for mindful listening and the comedic twists and turns that come with it.

The Mindful Melodrama Unfolds

You set out on a quest to practice mindfulness listening, armed with focus and a desire to truly hear others. You envision yourself as a listening guru, ready to give your full attention without any interruptions. Little do you know, the universe has some surprises in store for you.

The Mindful Misadventure

You attempt to practice mindfulness listening, hoping to be fully present for the speaker. But just as you start to tune in, your phone decides to chime with a barrage of notifications. You try to ignore it, but your curiosity gets the better of you. Before you know it, you're caught in a scrolling frenzy, completely forgetting about your quest for mindful listening.

The Listening Labyrinth

You try to give your full attention to the speaker, seeking to be fully engaged in the conversation. But just as you start to focus, your cat decides to join in with a series of meows that rival a TED talk. You try to maintain your concentration, but it's like trying to have a serious discussion in a cat café.

The Attention Avalanche

You strive to listen mindfully, recognizing the importance of being present in conversations. But just as you start to feel a sense of connection, your dog decides to join in with a series of howls that rival a motivational speaker. You try to keep your composure, but it's like trying to have a deep conversation in a dog park.

The Epiphany (Or Lack Thereof... Again)

After much effort and laughter, you finally have a moment of clarity. You realize that practicing mindfulness listening isn't just about being attentive—it's about finding humor in the human experience and laughing at life's absurdities. You might not achieve instant guru status, but you're okay with that. After all, life is a lot more fun when you're laughing at the absurdity of it all.

The Moral Of The Story

Practicing mindfulness listening, giving your full attention to the speaker without interrupting, is a journey that promises to bring connection and understanding to your relationships. It might not always go according to plan, and there might be some comedic mishaps along the way, but the effort is what counts. So, keep listening mindfully, keep laughing, and keep finding joy in the midst of life's mindful melodrama.

THE EMOTIONAL EXPEDITION

A Waggish Guide to Well-Being

Engaging in practices that promote emotional well-being, such as journaling and therapy, sounds like a journey to inner harmony. But let's face it—trying to find emotional balance in a world that sometimes feels like a comedy can be a bit like trying to have a serious conversation at a stand-up comedy show. Join us as we embark on a humorous exploration of the quest for emotional well-being and the comedic twists and turns that come with it.

The Emotional Excursion Begins

You set out on a quest to engage in practices that promote emotional well-being, armed with introspection and a desire for inner peace. You envision yourself as an emotional explorer, ready to navigate the ups and downs of life with grace and humor. Little do you know, the universe has some surprises in store for you.

The Journaling Journey

You attempt to practice journaling, hoping to process your emotions and gain clarity. But just as you start to pour your heart onto the page, your phone decides to chime with a barrage of notifications. You try to ignore it, but your curiosity gets the better of you. Before you know it, you're caught in a scrolling frenzy, completely forgetting about your quest for emotional release.

The Therapy Trial

You try to engage in therapy, seeking professional guidance to navigate your emotions. But just as you start to open up, your cat decides to join in with a series of meows that rival a therapy session. You try to maintain your focus, but it's like trying to have a breakthrough in a cat café.

The Emotional Ebb And Flow

You strive to promote emotional well-being, recognizing the importance of processing your feelings. But just as you start to feel a sense of peace, your dog decides to join in with a series of howls that rival a therapy breakthrough. You try to keep your composure, but it's like trying to find tranquility in a dog park.

The Epiphany (Or Lack Thereof... Again)

After much effort and laughter, you finally have a moment of clarity. You realize that engaging in practices that promote emotional well-being isn't just about finding balance—it's about finding humor in the human experience and laughing at life's absurdities. You might not achieve instant emotional enlightenment, but you're okay with that. After all, life is a lot more fun when you're laughing at the absurdity of it all.

The Moral Of The Story

Engaging in practices that promote emotional well-being, such as journaling and therapy, is a journey that promises to bring healing and self-discovery. It might not always go according to plan, and there might be some comedic mishaps along the way, but the effort is what counts. So, keep exploring your emotions, keep laughing, and keep finding joy in the midst of life's emotional expedition.

THE RESENTMENT RELEASE RODEO

A Playful Roundup of Letting Go

W elcome to the Resentment Release Rodeo, where we'll embark on a humorous journey through the practice of releasing any lingering resentments. Get ready for a wild ride of emotional acrobatics and inner cowpoke shenanigans as we wrangle with the art of letting go with a hearty laugh and a lasso of levity.

The Resentment Release Rodeo Rodeo

You saddle up for the rodeo of release, armed with a lasso of forgiveness and a cowboy hat of compassion. You envision yourself as a resentment wrangler, ready to corral your grudges with grit and humor. But as soon as you start to confront your resentments, they buck and kick like an ornery bronco.

The Resentment Release Rodeo Roundup

You attempt to practice releasing any lingering resentments, hoping to free yourself from the weight of past grievances. But just as you start to let go, your mind replays old arguments and injustices, dragging you back into the dusty arena of resentment like a bull with a bone to pick. You try to shake it off, but it's like trying to outrun a stampede.

The Resentment Release Rodeo Ruckus

You try to release lingering resentments, recognizing the freedom that comes with forgiveness. But just as you start to forgive, a memory of a past betrayal charges at you like a bull in a china shop, shattering your peace like a glassblower with a vendetta. You try to find your center, but it's like trying to ride a bucking bull blindfolded.

The Resentment Release Rodeo Reckoning

You strive to release any lingering resentments, understanding that it's a journey of healing and liberation. But just as you start to make progress, a voice in your head whispers doubts and fears, lassoing you back into the corral of bitterness like a cowboy with a grudge. You try to break free, but it's like trying to rope a tornado.

The Resentment Release Rodeo Revelry

After much effort and laughter, you finally have a moment of release. You realize that practicing letting go of lingering resentments isn't just about finding peace—it's about finding humor in the human experience and laughing at the absurdity of it all. You might not achieve instant wrangler status, but you're okay with that. After all, life is a lot more fun when you're laughing at the Resentment Release Rodeo of it all.

The Moral Of The Story

Practicing releasing any lingering resentments is a journey that promises to bring freedom and healing. It might not always go according to plan, and there might be some comedic mishaps along the way, but the effort is what counts. So, keep riding, keep laughing, and keep finding joy in the midst of life's Resentment Release Rodeo.

THE IMPERMANENCE INTERLUDE

A Farcical Guide to Living in the Now

Reflecting on the impermanence of life and the importance of living in the present moment sounds like a profound contemplation. But let's face it—trying to ponder the fleeting nature of existence in a world that sometimes feels like a comedy can be a bit like trying to have a serious conversation at a circus. Join us as we embark on a humorous exploration of the quest for present-moment awareness and the comedic twists and turns that come with it.

The Impermanence Inquiry Begins

You set out on a quest to reflect on the impermanence of life, armed with introspection and a desire to live in the now. You envision yourself as a present-moment sage, ready to embrace the fleeting nature of existence with grace and humor. Little do you know, the universe has some surprises in store for you.

The Fleeting Folly

You attempt to reflect on the impermanence of life, hoping to gain wisdom from the transient nature of all things. But just as you start to contemplate the ebb and flow of existence, your phone decides to chime with a barrage of notifications. You try to ignore it, but your curiosity gets the better of you. Before you know it, you're caught in a scrolling frenzy, completely forgetting about your quest for present-moment awareness.

The Now Nonsense

You try to live in the present moment, seeking to savor each fleeting experience. But just as you start to feel the joy of being present, your cat decides to join in with a series of meows that rival a mindfulness bell. You try to maintain your focus, but it's like trying to find peace in a cat café.

The Present Pantomime

You strive to embrace the impermanence of life, recognizing the beauty in each fleeting moment. But just as you start to feel a sense of acceptance, your dog decides to join in with a series of howls that rival a meditation chant. You try to keep your composure, but it's like trying to find stillness in a dog park.

The Epiphany (Or Lack Thereof... Again)

After much effort and laughter, you finally have a moment of clarity. You realize that reflecting on the impermanence of life and the importance of living in the present moment isn't just about finding peace—it's about finding humor in the human experience and laughing at life's absurdities. You might not achieve instant present-moment enlightenment, but you're okay with that. After all, life is a lot more fun when you're laughing at the absurdity of it all.

The Moral Of The Story

Reflecting on the impermanence of life and the importance of

living in the present moment is a journey that promises to bring mindfulness and appreciation to your life. It might not always go according to plan, and there might be some comedic mishaps along the way, but the effort is what counts. So, keep reflecting, keep laughing, and keep finding joy in the midst of life's impermanence interlude.

THE MINDFUL MUNCHIES

A Mirthful Guide to Savoring Food

Practicing mindfulness eating, savoring each bite and being present with your food, sounds like a delicious journey. But let's face it—trying to be mindful at mealtime in a world that sometimes feels like a comedy can be a bit like trying to have a serious conversation at a food fight. Join us as we embark on a humorous exploration of the quest for mindful eating and the comedic twists and turns that come with it.

The Mindful Munching Mission Begins

You set out on a quest to practice mindfulness eating, armed with a fork and a desire to savor every morsel. You envision yourself as a culinary connoisseur, ready to appreciate the flavors of life with gusto and humor. Little do you know, the universe has some surprises in store for you.

The Mindful Mealtime Mayhem

You attempt to practice mindfulness eating, hoping to savor each bite and be present with your food. But just as you start to tune into the flavors, your phone decides to chime with a barrage of notifications. You try to ignore it, but your curiosity gets the better of you. Before you know it, you're caught in a scrolling frenzy, completely forgetting about your quest for mindful munching.

The Savoring Shuffle

You try to savor each bite, seeking to appreciate the textures and tastes of your food. But just as you start to enjoy the culinary experience, your cat decides to join in with a series of meows that rival a cooking show. You try to maintain your focus, but it's like trying to find peace in a cat café.

The Culinary Comedy

You strive to be present with your food, recognizing the nourishment it provides for your body and soul. But just as you start to feel a sense of gratitude, your dog decides to join in with a series of howls that rival a gourmet feast. You try to keep your composure, but it's like trying to find tranquility in a dog park.

The Epiphany (Or Lack Thereof... Again)

After much effort and laughter, you finally have a moment of clarity. You realize that practicing mindfulness eating isn't just about savoring food—it's about finding humor in the human experience and laughing at life's absurdities. You might not achieve instant culinary enlightenment, but you're okay with that. After all, life is a lot more fun when you're laughing at the absurdity of it all.

The Moral Of The Story

Practicing mindfulness eating, savoring each bite and being present with your food, is a journey that promises to bring joy and appreciation to your meals. It might not always go according to plan, and there might be some comedic mishaps along the way, but the effort is what counts. So, keep savoring, keep laughing, and keep finding joy in the midst of life's mindful munchies.

THE WELL-BEING WHIMSY

A Zany Guide to Health

Engaging in practices that promote physical well-being, such as exercise and healthy eating, sounds like a journey to vitality. But let's face it—trying to stay healthy in a world that sometimes feels like a comedy can be a bit like trying to have a serious conversation at a fitness-themed party. Join us as we embark on a humorous exploration of the quest for physical well-being and the comedic twists and turns that come with it.

The Well-Being Whirlwind Begins

You set out on a quest to engage in practices that promote physical well-being, armed with determination and a desire for vitality. You envision yourself as a wellness warrior, ready to conquer the challenges of health with gusto and humor. Little do you know, the universe has some surprises in store for you.

The Exercise Escapade

You attempt to practice exercise, hoping to strengthen your body and boost your energy. But just as you start to feel the burn, your phone decides to chime with a barrage of notifications. You try to ignore it, but your curiosity gets the better of you. Before you know it, you're caught in a scrolling frenzy, completely forgetting about your quest for physical fitness.

The Healthy Eating Hijinks

You try to eat healthily, seeking to nourish your body with wholesome foods. But just as you start to enjoy your salad, your cat decides to join in with a series of meows that rival a cooking show. You try to maintain your focus, but it's like trying to have a gourmet meal in a cat café.

The Fitness Fiasco

You strive to promote physical well-being, recognizing the importance of regular exercise and nutritious eating. But just as you start to feel a sense of accomplishment, your dog decides to join in with a series of howls that rival a fitness instructor. You try to keep your composure, but it's like trying to find serenity in a dog park.

The Epiphany (Or Lack Thereof... Again)

After much effort and laughter, you finally have a moment of clarity. You realize that engaging in practices that promote physical well-being isn't just about staying healthy—it's about finding humor in the human experience and laughing at life's absurdities. You might not achieve instant wellness warrior status, but you're okay with that. After all, life is a lot more fun when you're laughing at the absurdity of it all.

The Moral Of The Story

Engaging in practices that promote physical well-being, such as exercise and healthy eating, is a journey that promises to bring vitality and joy to your life. It might not always go according to plan, and there might be some comedic mishaps along the way, but the effort is what counts. So, keep moving, keep nourishing, and keep finding joy in the midst of life's well-being whimsy.

THE FORGIVENESS FIASCO

An Entertaining Guide to
Self-Acceptance

Practicing forgiveness towards yourself for any past mistakes or shortcomings sounds like a journey to self-compassion. But let's face it—trying to forgive yourself in a world that sometimes feels like a comedy can be a bit like trying to have a serious conversation at a clown convention. Join us as we embark on a humorous exploration of the quest for self-forgiveness and the comedic twists and turns that come with it.

The Forgiveness Folly Begins

You set out on a quest to practice forgiveness towards yourself, armed with compassion and a desire for self-acceptance. You envision yourself as a forgiveness master, ready to let go of the past with grace and humor. Little do you know, the universe has some surprises in store for you.

The Mistake Mayhem

You attempt to practice forgiveness towards yourself, hoping to release any lingering guilt or shame. But just as you start to let go, your phone decides to chime with a barrage of notifications. You try to ignore it, but your curiosity gets the better of you. Before you know it, you're caught in a scrolling frenzy, completely forgetting about your quest for self-forgiveness.

The Shortcoming Shenanigans

You try to forgive yourself for any past shortcomings, seeking to embrace your imperfections with compassion. But just as you start to accept yourself, your cat decides to join in with a series of meows that rival a therapy session. You try to maintain your composure, but it's like trying to find peace in a cat café.

The Self-Acceptance Circus

You strive to practice self-forgiveness, recognizing that everyone makes mistakes and has shortcomings. But just as you start to feel a sense of liberation, your dog decides to join in with a series of howls that rival a self-help seminar. You try to keep your focus, but it's like trying to find clarity in a dog park.

The Epiphany (Or Lack Thereof... Again)

After much effort and laughter, you finally have a moment of clarity. You realize that practicing forgiveness towards yourself isn't just about letting go of the past—it's about finding humor in the human experience and laughing at life's absurdities. You might not achieve instant forgiveness guru status, but you're okay with that. After all, life is a lot more fun when you're laughing at the absurdity of it all.

The Moral Of The Story

Practicing forgiveness towards yourself for any past mistakes or shortcomings is a journey that promises to bring self-acceptance and peace to your life. It might not always go according to plan, and there might be some comedic mishaps along the way, but the effort is what counts. So, keep forgiving, keep laughing, and keep finding joy in the midst of life's forgiveness fiasco.

THE WEB OF LIFE WOBBLE

A Laughable Exploration of
Existential Entanglement

Welcome to the Web of Life Wobble, where we'll embark on a humorous journey through the reflection on your place in the interconnectedness of existence. Get ready for a cosmic comedy of errors and existential escapades as we navigate the tangled threads of the universe with a wink and a nod to the absurdity of it all.

The Web Of Life Wobble Wandering

You step into the cosmic chaos of interconnectedness, armed with a map of metaphysical musings and a compass of contemplation. You envision yourself as a navigator of the existential seas, ready to chart your course through the cosmic currents with wit and wisdom. But as soon as you start to ponder, your thoughts drift like cosmic dust in a solar wind.

The Web Of Life Wobble Weaving

You attempt to reflect on your place in the web of life, hoping to find meaning in the cosmic dance of existence. But just as you start to thread the needle of understanding, a distraction appears—a shooting star streaking across the sky, tempting you to make a wish like a child on a carnival ride. You try to refocus, but it's like trying to catch a comet with a butterfly net.

The Web Of Life Wobble Wonder

You try to reflect on your place in the web of life, recognizing the interconnectedness of all things. But just as you start to marvel at the cosmic symphony, a cloud passes over the moon, casting a shadow of doubt on your cosmic contemplations like a curtain on a stage. You try to see through the darkness, but it's like trying to find your way in a maze of mirrors.

The Web Of Life Wobble Worry

You strive to reflect on your place in the web of life, understanding that you are a small part of something much larger. But just as you start to embrace your cosmic insignificance, a thought creeps in—an existential crisis of cosmic proportions, questioning your place in the vastness of the universe like a flea on an elephant's back. You try to shake off the existential itch, but it's like trying to scratch an itch in a spacesuit.

The Web Of Life Wobble Wisdom

After much effort and laughter, you finally have a moment of cosmic clarity. You realize that reflecting on your place in the web of life isn't just about finding meaning—it's about finding humor in the cosmic absurdity and laughing at the grand cosmic joke. You might not solve the mystery of existence, but you're okay with that. After all, life is a lot more fun when you're laughing at the Web of Life Wobble of it all.

The Moral Of The Story

Reflecting on your place in the web of life is a journey that promises to bring insight and awe. It might not always go according to plan, and there might be some cosmic mishaps along the way, but the effort is what counts. So, keep pondering, keep laughing, and keep finding joy in the midst of life's Web of Life Wobble.

THE GRATITUDE GATHERING

A Jovial Guide to Thankfulness

Practicing gratitude for the abundance in your life, both material and spiritual, sounds like a journey to appreciation. But let's face it—trying to be grateful in a world that sometimes feels like a comedy can be a bit like trying to have a serious conversation at a gratitude-themed party. Join us as we embark on a humorous exploration of the quest for thankfulness and the comedic twists and turns that come with it.

The Gratitude Gathering Begins

You set out on a quest to practice gratitude for the abundance in your life, armed with appreciation and a desire to count your blessings. You envision yourself as a gratitude guru, ready to embrace the richness of life with grace and humor. Little do you know, the universe has some surprises in store for you.

The Abundance Affair

You attempt to practice gratitude for the material and spiritual abundance in your life, hoping to cultivate a sense of appreciation. But just as you start to feel thankful, your phone decides to chime with a barrage of notifications. You try to ignore it, but your curiosity gets the better of you. Before you know it, you're caught in a scrolling frenzy, completely forgetting about your quest for gratitude.

The Thankfulness Tango

You try to be grateful for the abundance in your life, recognizing the wealth of blessings that surround you. But just as you start to feel the warmth of gratitude, your cat decides to join in with a series of meows that rival a purring symphony. You try to maintain your composure, but it's like trying to find peace in a cat café.

The Gratitude Gathering

You strive to practice gratitude for both the material and spiritual abundance in your life, seeking to celebrate the richness of existence. But just as you start to feel a sense of abundance, your dog decides to join in with a series of howls that rival a symphony orchestra. You try to keep your focus, but it's like trying to find harmony in a dog park.

The Epiphany (Or Lack Thereof... Again)

After much effort and laughter, you finally have a moment of gratitude. You realize that practicing gratitude for the abundance in your life isn't just about counting blessings—it's about finding humor in the human experience and laughing at life's absurdities. You might not achieve instant gratitude guru status, but you're okay with that. After all, life is a lot more fun when you're laughing at the absurdity of it all.

The Moral Of The Story

Practicing gratitude for the abundance in your life, both material and spiritual, is a journey that promises to bring joy and appreciation to your life. It might not always go according to plan, and there might be some comedic mishaps along the way, but the effort is what counts. So, keep counting your blessings, keep laughing, and keep finding joy in the midst of life's gratitude gala.

THE CREATIVITY CIRCUS

A Humorous Guide to Expression

Engaging in activities that nurture your creativity and allow you to express yourself sounds like a journey to artistic freedom. But let's face it—trying to be creative in a world that sometimes feels like a comedy can be a bit like trying to have a serious conversation at an art-themed carnival. Join us as we embark on a humorous exploration of the quest for creative expression and the comedic twists and turns that come with it.

The Creativity Circus Commences

You set out on a quest to engage in activities that nurture your creativity, armed with inspiration and a desire for artistic expression. You envision yourself as a creativity connoisseur, ready to unleash your imagination with flair and humor. Little do you know, the universe has some surprises in store for you.

The Artistic Adventure

You attempt to practice creativity, hoping to unleash your artistic spirit. But just as you start to dive into your creative project, your phone decides to chime with a barrage of notifications. You try to ignore it, but your curiosity gets the better of you. Before you know it, you're caught in a scrolling frenzy, completely forgetting about your quest for creative inspiration.

The Expressive Extravaganza

You try to nurture your creativity, seeking activities that allow you to express yourself. But just as you start to get into the flow, your cat decides to join in with a series of meows that rival a poetry reading. You try to maintain your focus, but it's like trying to find inspiration in a cat café.

The Creative Comedy

You strive to engage in creative activities, recognizing the importance of self-expression. But just as you start to feel the creative juices flowing, your dog decides to join in with a series of howls that rival a jazz performance. You try to keep your composure, but it's like trying to find inspiration in a dog park.

The Epiphany (Or Lack Thereof... Again)

After much effort and laughter, you finally have a moment of creative clarity. You realize that engaging in activities that nurture your creativity isn't just about artistic expression—it's about finding humor in the human experience and laughing at life's absurdities. You might not achieve instant creative genius status, but you're okay with that. After all, life is a lot more fun when you're laughing at the absurdity of it all.

The Moral Of The Story

Engaging in activities that nurture your creativity and allow you to express yourself is a journey that promises to bring artistic freedom and joy to your life. It might not always go according to plan, and there might be some comedic mishaps along the way, but the effort is what counts. So, keep creating, keep laughing, and keep finding joy in the midst of life's creativity circus.

THE ACCEPTANCE AFFAIR

A Funny Guide to Embracing Uniqueness

Practicing acceptance of yourself and others, recognizing that everyone is on their own unique journey, sounds like a journey to understanding. But let's face it—trying to be accepting in a world that sometimes feels like a comedy can be a bit like trying to have a serious conversation at a diversity-themed party. Join us as we embark on a humorous exploration of the quest for acceptance and the comedic twists and turns that come with it.

The Acceptance Adventure Begins

You set out on a quest to practice acceptance of yourself and others, armed with empathy and a desire for understanding. You envision yourself as an acceptance ambassador, ready to embrace diversity with grace and humor. Little do you know, the universe has some surprises in store for you.

The Self-Acceptance Shuffle

You attempt to practice acceptance of yourself, hoping to embrace your quirks and imperfections. But just as you start to feel comfortable in your own skin, your phone decides to chime with a barrage of notifications. You try to ignore it, but your curiosity gets the better of you. Before you know it, you're caught in a scrolling frenzy, completely forgetting about your quest for self-acceptance.

The Diversity Dilemma

You try to be accepting of others, recognizing that everyone is on their own unique journey. But just as you start to appreciate diversity, your cat decides to join in with a series of meows that rival a multicultural celebration. You try to maintain your composure, but it's like trying to find harmony in a cat café.

The Uniqueness Uproar

You strive to practice acceptance of yourself and others, seeking to celebrate the diversity of humanity. But just as you start to feel a sense of inclusivity, your dog decides to join in with a series of howls that rival a unity rally. You try to keep your focus, but it's like trying to find understanding in a dog park.

The Epiphany (Or Lack Thereof... Again)

After much effort and laughter, you finally have a moment of acceptance. You realize that practicing acceptance of yourself and others isn't just about embracing diversity—it's about finding humor in the human experience and laughing at life's absurdities. You might not achieve instant acceptance ambassador status, but you're okay with that. After all, life is a lot more fun when you're laughing at the absurdity of it all.

The Moral Of The Story

Practicing acceptance of yourself and others, recognizing that everyone is on their own unique journey, is a journey that promises to bring understanding and compassion to your life. It might not always go according to plan, and there might be some comedic mishaps along the way, but the effort is what counts. So, keep accepting, keep laughing, and keep finding joy in the midst of life's acceptance affair.

THE ADMIRATION
ADVENTURE

An Amusing Guide to
Emulating Excellence

Reflecting on the qualities you admire in others and how you can cultivate them in yourself sounds like a journey to personal growth. But let's face it—trying to emulate excellence in a world that sometimes feels like a comedy can be a bit like trying to have a serious conversation at an admiration-themed party. Join us as we embark on a humorous exploration of the quest for self-improvement and the comedic twists and turns that come with it.

The Admiration Odyssey Begins

You set out on a quest to reflect on the qualities you admire in others, armed with introspection and a desire for personal growth. You envision yourself as an excellence explorer, ready to uncover the secrets of success with grace and humor. Little do you know, the universe has some surprises in store for you.

The Excellence Examination

You attempt to reflect on the qualities you admire in others, hoping to learn from their example. But just as you start to ponder their virtues, your phone decides to chime with a barrage of notifications. You try to ignore it, but your curiosity gets the better of you. Before you know it, you're caught in a scrolling frenzy, completely forgetting about your quest for self-improvement.

The Virtue Voyage

You try to cultivate the qualities you admire in others, seeking to incorporate their virtues into your own life. But just as you start to emulate their excellence, your cat decides to join in with a series of meows that rival a motivational speaker. You try to maintain your focus, but it's like trying to find inspiration in a cat café.

The Self-Improvement Spectacle

You strive to cultivate the qualities you admire in others, recognizing the potential for growth within yourself. But just as you start to feel a sense of progress, your dog decides to join in with a series of howls that rival a personal development seminar. You try to keep your composure, but it's like trying to find enlightenment in a dog park.

The Epiphany (Or Lack Thereof... Again)

After much effort and laughter, you finally have a moment of self-improvement insight. You realize that reflecting on the qualities you admire in others and how you can cultivate them in yourself isn't just about personal growth—it's about finding humor in the human experience and laughing at life's absurdities. You might not achieve instant excellence explorer status, but you're okay with that. After all, life is a lot more fun when you're laughing at the absurdity of it all.

The Moral Of The Story

Reflecting on the qualities you admire in others and how you can cultivate them in yourself is a journey that promises to bring growth and inspiration to your life. It might not always go according to plan, and there might be some comedic mishaps along the way, but the effort is what counts. So, keep reflecting, keep laughing, and keep finding joy in the midst of life's admiration adventure.

THE MINDFUL MOTORCADE

A Witty Guide to Zen Driving

Practicing mindfulness driving, staying present and focused on the road, sounds like a journey to serene commuting. But let's face it—trying to stay calm and focused behind the wheel in a world that sometimes feels like a comedy can be a bit like trying to have a serious conversation at a traffic jam. Join us as we embark on a humorous exploration of the quest for mindful driving and the comedic twists and turns that come with it.

The Mindful Motorcade Begins

You set out on a quest to practice mindfulness driving, armed with patience and a desire for peaceful commuting. You envision yourself as a zen driver, ready to navigate the roads with tranquility and humor. Little do you know, the universe has some surprises in store for you.

The Calm Commute Conundrum

You attempt to practice mindfulness driving, hoping to stay present and focused on the road. But just as you start to tune into the traffic, your phone decides to chime with a barrage of notifications. You try to ignore it, but your curiosity gets the better of you. Before you know it, you're caught in a scrolling frenzy, completely forgetting about your quest for zen driving.

The Road Rage Rumble

You try to stay present and focused on the road, seeking to navigate with ease. But just as you start to feel the zen vibes, another driver cuts you off with a move that rivals a Formula 1 race. You try to maintain your composure, but it's like trying to find peace in a rush-hour commute.

The Traffic Jam Tango

You strive to practice mindfulness driving, recognizing the importance of staying calm in traffic. But just as you start to embrace the slow pace, your cat decides to join in with a series of meows that rival a car horn symphony. You try to keep your focus, but it's like trying to find serenity in a cat café.

The Epiphany (Or Lack Thereof... Again)

After much effort and laughter, you finally have a moment of driving clarity. You realize that practicing mindfulness driving isn't just about staying calm on the road—it's about finding humor in the human experience and laughing at life's absurdities. You might not achieve instant zen driver status, but you're okay with that. After all, life is a lot more fun when you're laughing at the absurdity of it all.

The Moral Of The Story

Practicing mindfulness driving, staying present and focused on the road, is a journey that promises to bring peace and patience to your commute. It might not always go according to plan, and there might be some comedic mishaps along the way, but the effort is what counts. So, keep driving mindfully, keep laughing, and keep finding joy in the midst of life's mindful motorcade.

THE FOCUS FUNHOUSE

A Hilarious Carnival of Concentration

W elcome to the Focus Funhouse, where we'll embark on a humorous journey through practices that promote focus. Get ready for a wild ride of attention exercises and concentration capers as we navigate the carnival of concentration with a grin and a giggle at the tricks of distraction.

The Focus Funhouse Entrance

You step into the carnival of concentration, armed with a ticket of determination and a map of mindfulness. You envision yourself as a master of focus, ready to tackle the challenges of distraction with a sharp mind and a sense of humor. But as soon as you enter, your thoughts start to wander like a lost balloon in a gust of wind.

The Focus Funhouse Maze

You attempt to engage in practices that promote focus, hoping to sharpen your attention skills. But just as you start to concentrate, a maze appears—a labyrinth of distractions and dead ends that confuses your senses like a funhouse mirror. You try to find your way, but it's like trying to solve a puzzle in a hall of mirrors.

The Focus Funhouse Illusion

You try to practice focus, recognizing the importance of staying present. But just as you start to focus, an illusion appears—a magician performing tricks of misdirection that confuse your senses like a sleight of hand. You try to see through the illusion, but it's like trying to catch a magician's disappearing act.

The Focus Funhouse Distraction

You strive to engage in practices that promote focus, understanding that distractions can derail your efforts. But just as you start to concentrate, a clown appears—a jester of chaos that disrupts your thoughts like a prankster at a party. You try to ignore the clown, but it's like trying to silence a room full of laughter.

The Focus Funhouse Triumph

After much effort and laughter, you finally triumph in the Focus Funhouse. You realize that practicing focus isn't just about avoiding distractions—it's about finding humor in the challenges and laughing at the tricks of the mind. You might not achieve perfect concentration, but you're okay with that. After all, life is a lot more fun when you're laughing at the Focus Funhouse of it all.

The Moral Of The Story

Engaging in practices that promote focus is a journey that promises to bring mindfulness and attention skills. It might not always go according to plan, and there might be some comedic mishaps along the way, but the effort is what counts. So, keep practicing, keep laughing, and keep finding joy in the midst of life's Focus Funhouse.

THE GRATEFUL GIMMICK

A Comical Guide to
Embracing Challenges

Practicing gratitude for the challenges in your life, recognizing them as opportunities for growth, sounds like a journey to resilience. But let's face it—trying to be grateful for challenges in a world that sometimes feels like a comedy can be a bit like trying to have a serious conversation at a resilience-themed party. Join us as we embark on a humorous exploration of the quest for gratitude amidst challenges and the comedic twists and turns that come with it.

The Gratitude Gauntlet Begins

You set out on a quest to practice gratitude for the challenges in your life, armed with resilience and a desire for growth. You envision yourself as a gratitude guru, ready to embrace adversity with grace and humor. Little do you know, the universe has some surprises in store for you.

The Challenge Conundrum

You attempt to practice gratitude for the challenges in your life, hoping to find silver linings in adversity. But just as you start to see the lessons in your struggles, your phone decides to chime with a barrage of notifications. You try to ignore it, but your curiosity gets the better of you. Before you know it, you're caught in a scrolling frenzy, completely forgetting about your quest for gratitude.

The Resilience Riddle

You try to be grateful for the challenges in your life, recognizing them as opportunities for growth. But just as you start to embrace the ups and downs, your cat decides to join in with a series of meows that rival a motivational speech. You try to maintain your composure, but it's like trying to find positivity in a cat café.

The Adversity Adventure

You strive to practice gratitude for the challenges in your life, seeking to cultivate resilience. But just as you start to feel a sense of strength, your dog decides to join in with a series of howls that rival a pep rally. You try to keep your focus, but it's like trying to find motivation in a dog park.

The Epiphany (Or Lack Thereof... Again)

After much effort and laughter, you finally have a moment of gratitude. You realize that practicing gratitude for the challenges in your life isn't just about finding silver linings—it's about finding humor in the human experience and laughing at life's absurdities. You might not achieve instant gratitude guru status, but you're okay with that. After all, life is a lot more fun when you're laughing at the absurdity of it all.

The Moral Of The Story

Practicing gratitude for the challenges in your life, recognizing

them as opportunities for growth, is a journey that promises to bring resilience and wisdom to your life. It might not always go according to plan, and there might be some comedic mishaps along the way, but the effort is what counts. So, keep embracing challenges, keep laughing, and keep finding joy in the midst of life's grateful gag.

THE INTERCONNECTED INTERVAL

A Lighthearted Guide to Butterfly Effects and Cosmic Clarity

Reflecting on the interconnectedness of all beings and the impact of your actions on others sounds like a journey to cosmic enlightenment. But let's face it—trying to ponder the universe in a world that sometimes feels like a comedy can be a bit like trying to have a serious conversation at a cosmic comedy club. Join us as we embark on a humorous exploration of the quest for cosmic connection and the comedic twists and turns that come with it.

The Cosmic Connection Conundrum

You set out on a quest to reflect on the interconnectedness of all beings, armed with curiosity and a desire for cosmic clarity. You envision yourself as a cosmic detective, ready to unravel the mysteries of the universe with wit and humor. Little do you know, the universe has some surprises in store for you.

The Butterfly Effect Extravaganza

You attempt to reflect on the interconnectedness of all beings, hoping to understand the ripple effects of your actions. But just as you start to contemplate the cosmic web of cause and effect, your phone decides to chime with a barrage of notifications. You try to ignore it, but your curiosity gets the better of you. Before you know it, you're caught in a scrolling frenzy, completely forgetting about your quest for cosmic insight.

The Cosmic Comedy Club

You strive to grasp the interconnectedness of all beings, recognizing the intricate dance of life. But just as you start to feel a sense of interconnectedness, your cat decides to join in with a series of meows that rival a stand-up comedy routine. You try to maintain your focus, but it's like trying to find enlightenment in a cat café.

The Cosmic Clarity (Or Lack Thereof... Again)

After much effort and laughter, you finally have a moment of cosmic clarity. You realize that reflecting on the interconnectedness of all beings isn't just about cosmic wisdom —it's about finding humor in the human experience and laughing at life's absurdities. You might not achieve instant enlightenment, but you're okay with that. After all, life is a lot more fun when you're laughing at the absurdity of it all.

The Moral Of The Story

Reflecting on the interconnectedness of all beings and the impact of your actions on others is a journey that promises to bring insight and wonder to your life. It might not always go according to plan, and there might be some comedic mishaps along the way, but the effort is what counts. So, keep reflecting, keep laughing, and keep finding joy in the midst of life's cosmic comedy club.

THE MINDFUL MELTDOWN

A Jocular Guide to Listening Without Losing It

Practicing mindfulness listening, giving your full attention to the speaker without interrupting, sounds like a journey to attentive communication. But let's face it—trying to be fully present in a world that sometimes feels like a comedy can be a bit like trying to have a serious conversation at a talk show taping. Join us as we embark on a humorous exploration of the quest for mindful listening and the comedic twists and turns that come with it.

The Mindful Listening Mission Begins

You set out on a quest to practice mindfulness listening, armed with patience and a desire for attentive communication. You envision yourself as a listening guru, ready to tune in with grace and humor. Little do you know, the universe has some surprises in store for you.

The Listening Labyrinth

You attempt to practice mindfulness listening, hoping to give your full attention to the speaker. But just as you start to focus, your phone decides to chime with a barrage of notifications. You try to ignore it, but your curiosity gets the better of you. Before you know it, you're caught in a scrolling frenzy, completely forgetting about your quest for mindful listening.

The Attention Apocalypse

You try to give your full attention to the speaker, recognizing the importance of mindful presence. But just as you start to engage, another voice joins the conversation with a volume that rivals a rock concert. You try to maintain your focus, but it's like trying to find silence in a crowded stadium.

The Mindful Meltdown

You strive to practice mindfulness listening, seeking to listen without interrupting. But just as you start to tune in, your cat decides to join in with a series of meows that rival a podcast host. You try to keep your composure, but it's like trying to find peace in a cat café.

The Epiphany (Or Lack Thereof... Again)

After much effort and laughter, you finally have a moment of mindful listening. You realize that practicing mindfulness listening isn't just about being attentive—it's about finding humor in the human experience and laughing at life's absurdities. You might not achieve instant listening guru status, but you're okay with that. After all, life is a lot more fun when you're laughing at the absurdity of it all.

The Moral Of The Story

Practicing mindfulness listening, giving your full attention to the speaker without interrupting, is a journey that promises to bring attentive communication and understanding to your interactions. It might not always go according to plan, and there might be some comedic mishaps along the way, but the effort is what counts. So, keep listening mindfully, keep laughing, and keep finding joy in the midst of life's mindful meltdown.

THE EMOTIONAL ESCAPADE

A Droll Guide to Well-Being Woes

Engaging in practices that promote emotional well-being, such as journaling and therapy, sounds like a journey to inner peace. But let's face it—trying to find balance in a world that sometimes feels like a comedy can be a bit like trying to have a serious conversation at a therapy-themed party. Join us as we embark on a humorous exploration of the quest for emotional well-being and the comedic twists and turns that come with it.

The Well-Being Wobble Begins

You set out on a quest to engage in practices that promote emotional well-being, armed with introspection and a desire for inner peace. You envision yourself as an emotional explorer, ready to navigate the ups and downs of life with grace and humor. Little do you know, the universe has some surprises in store for you.

The Journaling Jamboree

You attempt to practice journaling, hoping to process your emotions and gain clarity. But just as you start to pour your heart out onto the page, your phone decides to chime with a barrage of notifications. You try to ignore it, but your curiosity gets the better of you. Before you know it, you're caught in a scrolling frenzy, completely forgetting about your quest for emotional well-being.

The Therapy Tango

You try to engage in therapy, seeking professional guidance and support. But just as you start to open up, your cat decides to join in with a series of meows that rival a therapy session. You try to maintain your focus, but it's like trying to find peace in a cat café.

The Well-Being Whirlwind

You strive to engage in practices that promote emotional well-being, recognizing the importance of self-care. But just as you start to feel a sense of calm, your dog decides to join in with a series of howls that rival a meditation session. You try to keep your composure, but it's like trying to find tranquility in a dog park.

The Epiphany (Or Lack Thereof... Again)

After much effort and laughter, you finally have a moment of emotional well-being. You realize that engaging in practices that promote emotional well-being isn't just about finding peace—it's about finding humor in the human experience and laughing at life's absurdities. You might not achieve instant inner peace, but you're okay with that. After all, life is a lot more fun when you're laughing at the absurdity of it all.

The Moral Of The Story

Engaging in practices that promote emotional well-being, such as journaling and therapy, is a journey that promises to bring balance and understanding to your life. It might not always go according to plan, and there might be some comedic mishaps along the way, but the effort is what counts. So, keep exploring your emotions, keep laughing, and keep finding joy in the midst of life's emotional escapade.

THE HOSTILITY HOUDINI

A Whimsical Escape from Anger

Welcome to The Hostility Houdini, where we'll embark on a humorous journey through the practice of releasing any lingering hostility. Get ready for a magical escapade of anger management tricks and laughter therapy as we make anger disappear with a wave of our wands and a wink of our eyes.

The Hostility Houdini Setup

You step into the arena of anger management, armed with a wand of peace and a hat of humor. You envision yourself as a magician of tranquility, ready to perform the ultimate disappearing act with your anger. But as soon as you take the stage, your emotions start to boil like a cauldron of potions gone awry.

The Hostility Houdini Illusion

You attempt to practice releasing any lingering hostility, hoping to let go of your anger. But just as you start to relax, an illusion appears—a mirage of past grievances that threatens to cloud your judgment like a fog over a river. You try to see through it, but it's like trying to find a needle in a haystack.

The Hostility Houdini Misdirection

You try to practice releasing any lingering hostility, recognizing the importance of forgiveness. But just as you start to forgive, a misdirection appears—a distraction that pulls your attention away from your goal like a magician's sleight of hand. You try to stay focused, but it's like trying to catch a magician in the act.

The Hostility Houdini Disappearance

You strive to practice releasing any lingering hostility, understanding that holding onto anger only hurts you. But just as you start to let go, a disappearance appears—a moment of clarity that allows you to see the futility of your anger like a spotlight in the darkness. You try to embrace it, but it's like trying to hold onto water.

The Hostility Houdini Reappearance

After much effort and laughter, you finally achieve The Hostility Houdini. You realize that practicing releasing any lingering hostility isn't just about letting go—it's about finding humor in the process and laughing at the absurdity of holding onto anger. You might not always make your anger disappear, but you're okay with that. After all, life is a lot more magical when you're laughing at The Hostility Houdini of it all.

The Moral Of The Story

Practicing releasing any lingering hostility is a journey that promises to bring peace and freedom from anger. It might not always go according to plan, and there might be some comedic mishaps along the way, but the effort is what counts. So, keep practicing, keep laughing, and keep finding joy in the midst of life's Hostility Houdini.

THE IMPERMANENT IMPROV

A Comedic Guide to Embracing Change

Reflecting on the impermanence of life and the importance of living in the present moment sounds like a journey to mindfulness. But let's face it—trying to contemplate existence in a world that sometimes feels like a comedy can be a bit like trying to have a serious conversation at an impermanence-themed party. Join us as we embark on a humorous exploration of the quest for mindfulness and the comedic twists and turns that come with it.

The Mindful Musing Begins

You set out on a quest to reflect on the impermanence of life, armed with introspection and a desire for presence. You envision yourself as a mindfulness master, ready to embrace change with grace and humor. Little do you know, the universe has some surprises in store for you.

The Impermanence Interlude

You attempt to reflect on the impermanence of life, hoping to find wisdom in the transient nature of existence. But just as you start to contemplate the fleeting moments, your phone decides to chime with a barrage of notifications. You try to ignore it, but your curiosity gets the better of you. Before you know it, you're caught in a scrolling frenzy, completely forgetting about your quest for mindfulness.

The Present Moment Paradox

You try to live in the present moment, recognizing the importance of cherishing each experience. But just as you start to savor the now, another voice joins the conversation with a volume that rivals a concert. You try to maintain your focus, but it's like trying to find silence in a crowded stadium.

The Impermanent Improv

You strive to embrace the impermanence of life, seeking to find peace in change. But just as you start to feel a sense of acceptance, your cat decides to join in with a series of meows that rival a philosophical debate. You try to keep your composure, but it's like trying to find tranquility in a cat café.

The Epiphany (Or Lack Thereof... Again)

After much effort and laughter, you finally have a moment of mindfulness. You realize that reflecting on the impermanence of life isn't just about finding wisdom—it's about finding humor in the human experience and laughing at life's absurdities. You might not achieve instant mindfulness master status, but you're okay with that. After all, life is a lot more fun when you're laughing at the absurdity of it all.

The Moral Of The Story

Reflecting on the impermanence of life and the importance of living in the present moment is a journey that promises to bring mindfulness and acceptance to your life. It might not always go according to plan, and there might be some comedic mishaps along the way, but the effort is what counts. So, keep reflecting, keep laughing, and keep finding joy in the midst of life's impermanent improv.

THE MINDFUL APPETITE

A Waggish Guide to
Chew and Chortle

Practicing mindfulness eating, savoring each bite and being present with your food, sounds like a journey to culinary consciousness. But let's face it—trying to eat mindfully in a world that sometimes feels like a comedy can be a bit like trying to have a serious conversation at a food-themed stand-up show. Join us as we embark on a humorous exploration of the quest for mindful eating and the comedic twists and turns that come with it.

The Mindful Appetite Mission Begins

You set out on a quest to practice mindfulness eating, armed with hunger and a desire for gastronomic enlightenment. You envision yourself as a foodie philosopher, ready to savor each morsel with grace and humor. Little do you know, the universe has some surprises in store for you.

The Mindful Mealtime

You attempt to practice mindfulness eating, hoping to fully experience the flavors and textures of your food. But just as you start to savor the first bite, your phone decides to chime with a barrage of notifications. You try to ignore it, but your curiosity gets the better of you. Before you know it, you're caught in a scrolling frenzy, completely forgetting about your quest for mindful eating.

The Gastronomic Gag

You try to be present with your food, recognizing the importance of enjoying each moment. But just as you start to appreciate the culinary masterpiece in front of you, another voice joins the conversation with a volume that rivals a cooking show. You try to maintain your focus, but it's like trying to find peace in a crowded kitchen.

The Mindful Appetite Mayhem

You strive to engage in practices that promote mindfulness eating, seeking to find joy in every bite. But just as you start to feel a sense of culinary bliss, your dog decides to join in with a series of howls that rival a gourmet meal. You try to keep your composure, but it's like trying to find tranquility in a dog park.

The Epiphany (Or Lack Thereof... Again)

After much effort and laughter, you finally have a moment of mindful eating. You realize that practicing mindfulness eating isn't just about savoring flavors—it's about finding humor in the human experience and laughing at life's absurdities. You might not achieve instant culinary enlightenment, but you're okay with that. After all, life is a lot more fun when you're laughing at the absurdity of it all.

The Moral Of The Story

Practicing mindfulness eating, savoring each bite and being

present with your food, is a journey that promises to bring joy and appreciation to your meals. It might not always go according to plan, and there might be some comedic mishaps along the way, but the effort is what counts. So, keep munching mindfully, keep laughing, and keep finding joy in the midst of life's culinary comedy.

THE WELLNESS WOBBLE

A Playful Guide to Fitness Follies

E ngaging in practices that promote physical well-being, such as exercise and healthy eating, sounds like a journey to fitness nirvana. But let's face it—trying to stay healthy in a world that sometimes feels like a comedy can be a bit like trying to have a serious workout at a fitness-themed amusement park. Join us as we embark on a humorous exploration of the quest for physical well-being and the comedic twists and turns that come with it.

The Wellness Workout Begins

You set out on a quest to engage in practices that promote physical well-being, armed with determination and a desire for fitness. You envision yourself as a wellness warrior, ready to conquer the challenges of health with grace and humor. Little do you know, the universe has some surprises in store for you.

The Exercise Expedition

You attempt to exercise regularly, hoping to stay fit and healthy. But just as you start to feel the burn, your phone decides to chime with a barrage of notifications. You try to ignore it, but your curiosity gets the better of you. Before you know it, you're caught in a scrolling frenzy, completely forgetting about your quest for physical well-being.

The Healthy Eating Hurdle

You try to eat healthily, recognizing the importance of nourishing your body. But just as you start to enjoy your salad, another voice joins the meal with a volume that rivals a food competition. You try to maintain your focus, but it's like trying to find peace in a crowded cafeteria.

The Wellness Whirlwind

You strive to engage in practices that promote physical well-being, seeking to find balance in your lifestyle. But just as you start to feel a sense of accomplishment, your cat decides to join in with a series of meows that rival a workout playlist. You try to keep your composure, but it's like trying to find tranquility in a cat café.

The Epiphany (Or Lack Thereof... Again)

After much effort and laughter, you finally have a moment of physical well-being. You realize that engaging in practices that promote physical well-being isn't just about staying fit— it's about finding humor in the human experience and laughing at life's absurdities. You might not achieve instant wellness warrior status, but you're okay with that. After all, life is a lot more fun when you're laughing at the absurdity of it all.

The Moral Of The Story

Engaging in practices that promote physical well being, such as exercise and healthy eating, is a journey that promises to bring fitness and vitality to your life. It might not always go according to plan, and there might be some comedic mishaps along the way, but the effort is what counts. So, keep exercising, keep eating healthily, keep laughing, and keep finding joy in the midst of life's wellness wobble.

THE SHORTCOMING SHUFFLE

A Farcical Concoction of Embracing Imperfection

Welcome to the Shortcoming Shuffle, where we'll embark on a humorous journey through the practice of letting go of shortcomings. Get ready for a lively dance of self-acceptance and lightheartedness as we shimmy through the steps of imperfection with a skip in our stride and a twirl of laughter.

The Shortcoming Shuffle Prelude

You step onto the dance floor of self-acceptance, armed with a playlist of positivity and a pair of dancing shoes of determination. You envision yourself as a master of the imperfect waltz, ready to twirl through life's missteps with grace and humor. But as soon as you start to move, your feet trip over each other like a clumsy foxtrot.

The Shortcoming Shuffle Samba

You attempt to practice letting go of shortcomings, hoping to embrace your imperfections with open arms. But just as you start to sway to the rhythm of self-acceptance, your mind starts to play a discordant tune of self-criticism, throwing off your groove like a jazz band in a heavy metal concert. You try to find your rhythm, but it's like trying to salsa in cement shoes.

The Shortcoming Shuffle Cha-Cha

You try to let go of shortcomings, recognizing that perfection is an illusion. But just as you start to find your groove, a memory of past failures creeps in, stepping on your toes like a clumsy tango partner. You try to lead the dance, but it's like trying to waltz with a partner who has two left feet.

The Shortcoming Shuffle Jive

You strive to let go of shortcomings, understanding that it's a dance of self-compassion and growth. But just as you start to spin with joy, a voice in your head whispers doubts and insecurities, throwing off your balance like a breakdancer on a tightrope. You try to keep your rhythm, but it's like trying to moonwalk on a treadmill.

The Shortcoming Shuffle Shimmy

After much effort and laughter, you finally find your rhythm. You realize that practicing letting go of shortcomings isn't just about embracing imperfection—it's about finding humor in the human experience and laughing at the absurdity of it all. You might not achieve instant dancer status, but you're okay with that. After all, life is a lot more fun when you're laughing at the Shortcoming Shuffle of it all.

The Moral Of The Story

Practicing letting go of shortcomings is a dance that promises to bring self-acceptance and growth. It might not always go according to plan, and there might be some comedic mishaps along the way, but the effort is what counts. So, keep dancing, keep laughing, and keep finding joy in the midst of life's Shortcoming Shuffle.

THE INTERCONNECTED
INTERMISSION

A Zany Guide to Existential Entanglement

Reflecting on the interconnectedness of all things and your place in the web of life sounds like a journey to ponder the profound. But let's face it—trying to unravel the mysteries of existence in a world that sometimes feels like a comedy can be a bit like trying to have a serious discussion at a cosmic comedy club. Join us as we embark on a humorous exploration of the quest for existential enlightenment and the comedic twists and turns that come with it.

The Cosmic Curtain Rises

You set out on a quest to reflect on the interconnectedness of all things, armed with wonder and a desire for cosmic clarity. You envision yourself as a philosophical jester, ready to dance through the cosmos with grace and humor. Little do you know, the universe has some cosmic comedy in store for you.

The Interconnected Inquiry

You attempt to reflect on the interconnectedness of all things, hoping to grasp the cosmic dance. But just as you start to contemplate the cosmic ballet, your phone decides to chime with a barrage of notifications. You try to ignore it, but your curiosity gets the better of you. Before you know it, you're caught in a scrolling vortex, completely forgetting about your quest for cosmic connection.

The Universal Uproar

You try to contemplate your place in the web of life, recognizing the vastness of the cosmos. But just as you start to feel a sense of cosmic insignificance, another voice joins the cosmic chorus with a volume that rivals a supernova's explosion. You try to maintain your cosmic perspective, but it's like trying to find stillness in a cosmic storm.

The Cosmic Comedy Hour

You strive to engage in practices that promote cosmic connection, seeking to find harmony in the cosmic symphony. But just as you start to feel a sense of cosmic unity, your cat decides to join in with a series of meows that rival a cosmic choir. You try to keep your cosmic composure, but it's like trying to find tranquility in a cat café.

The Cosmic Clarity (Or Lack Thereof... Again)

After much cosmic contemplation and laughter, you finally have a moment of cosmic connection. You realize that reflecting on the interconnectedness of all things isn't just about finding answers—it's about finding humor in the cosmic dance and laughing at life's cosmic absurdities. You might not achieve instant cosmic enlightenment, but you're okay with that. After all, life is a lot more fun when you're laughing at the cosmic comedy of it all.

The Moral Of The Cosmic Comedy

Reflecting on the interconnectedness of all things and your place in the web of life is a cosmic journey that promises to bring wonder and cosmic comedy to your existence. It might not always go according to plan, and there might be some cosmic mishaps along the way, but the cosmic effort is what counts. So, keep reflecting, keep laughing, and keep finding cosmic joy in the midst of life's interconnected intermission.

THE BLESSINGS BONANZA

A Mirthful Guide to Counting Blessings and Chuckling

P racticing gratitude for the abundance in your life, both material and spiritual, sounds like a journey to appreciate the riches of existence. But let's face it—trying to count your blessings in a world that sometimes feels like a comedy can be a bit like trying to have a serious conversation at a gratitude-themed carnival. Join us as we embark on a humorous exploration of the quest for gratitude and the comedic twists and turns that come with it.

The Blessing Bonanza Begins

You set out on a quest to practice gratitude for the abundance in your life, armed with appreciation and a desire for contentment. You envision yourself as a gratitude guru, ready to embrace life's blessings with grace and humor. Little do you know, the universe has some surprises in store for you.

The Gratitude Groove

You attempt to practice gratitude, hoping to cultivate a sense of abundance and joy. But just as you start to count your blessings, your phone decides to chime with a barrage of notifications. You try to ignore it, but your curiosity gets the better of you. Before you know it, you're caught in a scrolling frenzy, completely forgetting about your quest for gratitude.

The Abundance Antics

You try to appreciate the abundance in your life, recognizing the richness of your experiences. But just as you start to feel grateful, another voice joins the conversation with a volume that rivals a celebration. You try to maintain your focus, but it's like trying to find peace in a crowded party.

The Blessings Bonanza

You strive to engage in practices that promote gratitude, seeking to find joy in the simple things. But just as you start to feel a sense of gratitude, your cat decides to join in with a series of meows that rival a gratitude meditation. You try to keep your composure, but it's like trying to find tranquility in a cat café.

The Epiphany (Or Lack Thereof... Again)

After much effort and laughter, you finally have a moment of gratitude. You realize that practicing gratitude for the abundance in your life isn't just about counting blessings—it's about finding humor in the human experience and laughing at life's absurdities. You might not achieve instant gratitude guru status, but you're okay with that. After all, life is a lot more fun when you're laughing at the blessing bonanza of it all.

The Moral Of The Blessing Bonanza

Practicing gratitude for the abundance in your life, both material and spiritual, is a journey that promises to bring joy and appreciation to your life. It might not always go according to plan, and there might be some comedic mishaps along the way, but the effort is what counts. So, keep practicing gratitude, keep laughing, and keep finding joy in the midst of life's gratitude gala.

THE CREATIVITY CELEBRATION

An Entertaining Guide to Unleashing Your Imagination and Giggling

E ngaging in activities that nurture your creativity and allow you to express yourself sounds like a journey to artistic liberation. But let's face it—trying to unleash your imagination in a world that sometimes feels like a comedy can be a bit like trying to have a serious art class at a creativity-themed amusement park. Join us as we embark on a humorous exploration of the quest for creative expression and the comedic twists and turns that come with it.

The Creative Carnival Begins

You set out on a quest to engage in activities that nurture your creativity, armed with inspiration and a desire for artistic freedom. You envision yourself as a creative clown, ready to paint the canvas of life with bold strokes of humor and imagination. Little do you know, the universe has some surprises in store for you.

The Creative Chaos

You attempt to engage in creative activities, hoping to unleash your artistic potential. But just as you start to doodle your masterpiece, your phone decides to chime with a barrage of notifications. You try to ignore it, but your curiosity gets the better of you. Before you know it, you're caught in a scrolling frenzy, completely forgetting about your quest for creativity.

The Artistic Antics

You try to nurture your creativity, recognizing the importance of self-expression. But just as you start to immerse yourself in your creative project, another voice joins the artistic symphony with a volume that rivals a gallery opening. You try to maintain your focus, but it's like trying to find inspiration in a crowded art studio.

The Creative Carnival

You strive to engage in activities that promote creativity, seeking to unleash your inner artist. But just as you start to feel a surge of creative energy, your cat decides to join in with a series of meows that rival a creative brainstorming session. You try to keep your composure, but it's like trying to find tranquility in a cat café.

The Epiphany (Or Lack Thereof... Again)

After much creative chaos and laughter, you finally have a moment of artistic expression. You realize that engaging in activities that nurture your creativity isn't just about making art —it's about finding humor in the creative process and laughing at life's artistic absurdities. You might not achieve instant artistic mastery, but you're okay with that. After all, life is a lot more fun when you're laughing at the creativity celebration of it all.

The Moral Of The Creative Carnival

Engaging in activities that nurture your creativity and allow you to express yourself is a journey that promises to bring joy and artistic fulfillment to your life. It might not always go according to plan, and there might be some creative mishaps along the way, but the effort is what counts. So, keep creating, keep laughing, and keep finding joy in the midst of life's creative carnival.

THE ACCEPTANCE AMUSEMENT PARK

*A Laughable Guide to Embracing
Your Quirks and Chuckling
at Life's Eccentricities*

P racticing acceptance of yourself and others, recognizing that everyone is on their own unique journey, sounds like a journey to inner peace. But let's face it—trying to embrace your quirks in a world that sometimes feels like a comedy can be a bit like trying to have a serious conversation at an acceptance-themed amusement park. Join us as we embark on a humorous exploration of the quest for self-acceptance and the comedic twists and turns that come with it.

The Acceptance Adventure Begins

You set out on a quest to practice acceptance, armed with self-love and a desire for peace of mind. You envision yourself as an acceptance aficionado, ready to navigate the rollercoaster of life with grace and humor. Little do you know, the universe has some surprises in store for you.

The Self-Acceptance Safari

You attempt to practice self-acceptance, hoping to embrace your quirks and imperfections. But just as you start to appreciate your uniqueness, your phone decides to chime with a barrage of notifications. You try to ignore it, but your curiosity gets the better of you. Before you know it, you're caught in a scrolling frenzy, completely forgetting about your quest for self-acceptance.

The Eccentricity Extravaganza

You try to accept yourself, recognizing the beauty in your quirks. But just as you start to celebrate your individuality, another voice joins the conversation with a volume that rivals a carnival barker. You try to maintain your composure, but it's like trying to find tranquility in a crowded theme park.

The Acceptance Amusement

You strive to engage in practices that promote acceptance, seeking to embrace the diversity of human experience. But just as you start to feel a sense of acceptance, your cat decides to join in with a series of meows that rival a circus performance. You try to keep your composure, but it's like trying to find peace in a cat café.

The Epiphany (Or Lack Thereof... Again)

After much effort and laughter, you finally have a moment of self-acceptance. You realize that practicing acceptance of yourself and others isn't just about embracing quirks—it's about finding humor in the human experience and laughing at life's eccentricities. You might not achieve instant acceptance aficionado status, but you're okay with that. After all, life is a lot more fun when you're laughing at the acceptance amusement park of it all.

The Moral Of The Story

Practicing acceptance of yourself and others, recognizing that everyone is on their own unique journey, is a journey that promises to bring peace and understanding to your life. It might not always go according to plan, and there might be some comedic mishaps along the way, but the effort is what counts. So, keep accepting, keep laughing, and keep finding joy in the midst of life's acceptance adventure.

THE QUALITY QUANDARY

A Jovial Quest for Self-Improvement

Welcome to the Quality Quandary, where we'll embark on a humorous journey through the reflection on the qualities you admire in others and how you can cultivate them in yourself. Get ready for a comedic exploration of personal development and character quirks as we navigate the landscape of virtue with a chuckle and a dash of whimsy.

The Quality Quandary Quest

You set out on a quest for self-improvement, armed with a checklist of admirable qualities and a magnifying glass of introspection. You envision yourself as a character in a quest for personal growth, ready to slay the dragons of doubt and conquer the mountains of mediocrity with wit and determination. But as soon as you start to examine your own qualities, your thoughts scatter like sheep in a thunderstorm.

The Quality Quandary Conundrum

You attempt to reflect on the qualities you admire in others, hoping to emulate their virtues. But just as you start to list the qualities, a distraction appears—a flock of birds flies by, distracting you with their graceful flight like a ballet troupe in the sky. You try to refocus, but it's like trying to herd cats in a hurricane.

The Quality Quandary Comedy

You try to reflect on the qualities you admire, recognizing the value of self-improvement. But just as you start to brainstorm ways to cultivate those qualities, a voice in your head starts to doubt your abilities, whispering self-deprecating remarks like a stand-up comedian with a heckler in the audience. You try to silence the inner critic, but it's like trying to perform a magic trick with a rabbit that refuses to disappear.

The Quality Quandary Capers

You strive to reflect on the qualities you admire in others, understanding that personal growth is a journey. But just as you start to brainstorm strategies for improvement, a memory of past failures creeps in, casting a shadow of doubt on your aspirations like a cloud on a sunny day. You try to chase away the clouds, but it's like trying to outrun your own shadow.

The Quality Quandary Conclusion

After much effort and laughter, you finally have a moment of insight. You realize that reflecting on the qualities you admire in others and how you can cultivate them in yourself isn't just about self-improvement—it's about finding humor in the quirks of character and laughing at the absurdity of it all. You might not achieve instant virtuosity, but you're okay with that. After all, life is a lot more fun when you're laughing at the Quality Quandary of it all.

The Moral Of The Story

Reflecting on the qualities you admire in others and how you can cultivate them in yourself is a journey that promises to bring growth and self-awareness. It might not always go according to plan, and there might be some comedic mishaps along the way, but the effort is what counts. So, keep reflecting, keep laughing, and keep finding joy in the midst of life's Quality Quandary.

THE MINDFUL MOTORWAY

A Humorous Guide to Staying Zen Behind the Wheel

B uckle up, because we're about to take a humorous spin through the world of mindful driving. Practicing mindfulness while driving, staying present and focused on the road, might sound like a serene journey, but in reality, it can be a bit like trying to have a peaceful picnic in the middle of a car wash. Let's navigate this comedic adventure together as we explore the highs and lows of staying zen behind the wheel.

The Zen Zone

You embark on your mindful driving journey with the determination of a Zen master, ready to stay present and focused on the road ahead. You imagine yourself as the epitome of tranquility, gliding through traffic with ease. But as soon as you hit the road, reality hits you like a rogue pothole. Horns blare, cars weave in and out of lanes like confused dancers, and your serene mindset is put to the ultimate test.

The Mindful Maneuver

You attempt to practice mindfulness, but it's hard to stay focused when the driver in front of you is applying makeup, the driver beside you is singing at the top of their lungs, and your

GPS is giving you conflicting directions like a backseat driver on steroids. You try to breathe deeply and find your inner calm, but it's like trying to meditate in the middle of a carnival.

The Road To Ruin

Just when you think you've mastered the art of mindfulness on the road, a traffic jam materializes out of nowhere, testing your patience like a cosmic joke. You try to maintain your composure, but the urge to scream into the void is overwhelming. You remind yourself that mindfulness is about accepting the present moment, even if that moment involves being stuck in traffic with a clown car behind you.

The Epiphany (Or Lack Thereof... Again)

After surviving the mindful motorway, you realize that practicing mindfulness while driving isn't just about staying focused—it's about finding humor in the chaos and embracing the absurdity of life on the road. You might not achieve instant zen behind the wheel, but you've learned to laugh at the unpredictable nature of driving and appreciate the moments of calm amidst the chaos.

The Moral Of The Story

Practicing mindfulness while driving is like trying to find stillness in a storm—it's not always easy, but it's worth the effort. So, next time you're behind the wheel, remember to breathe, stay present, and don't forget to laugh at the comedy of errors that is the mindful motorway.

THE CLARITY CARNIVAL

An Amusing Guide to
Clearing the Mental Fog and
Embracing Inner Peace

Welcome to the Clarity Carnival, where we'll take a humorous journey through the world of practices that promote mental clarity and focus. Get ready for a ride filled with meditation mishaps, deep breathing dilemmas, and plenty of laughter along the way.

The Clarity Quest Begins

You set out on your quest for mental clarity, armed with a yoga mat and a determination to find inner peace. You envision yourself as a zen master, effortlessly clearing the mental fog with each breath. But as you sit down to meditate, your mind starts to wander like a lost balloon at a carnival, and you find yourself thinking about everything from your grocery list to that embarrassing thing you said five years ago.

The Meditation Muddle

You attempt to meditate, hoping to quiet your mind and find focus. But just as you start to feel a sense of calm, your phone decides to chime with a barrage of notifications. You try to ignore it, but your curiosity gets the better of you. Before you know it, you're caught in a scrolling frenzy, completely forgetting about your quest for mental clarity.

The Deep Breathing Dilemma

You try to practice deep breathing, inhaling and exhaling with the rhythm of the ocean. But just as you start to feel the soothing effects of your breath, your cat decides to join in with a series of meows that rival a symphony orchestra. You try to keep your composure, but it's like trying to find peace in a cat café.

The Mindful Mayhem

You strive to engage in practices that promote mental clarity, seeking to find focus in a world full of distractions. But just as you start to feel a sense of clarity, your neighbor decides to mow their lawn with a mower that sounds like a chainsaw. You try to block out the noise, but it's like trying to find silence at a rock concert.

The Epiphany (Or Lack Thereof... Again)

After much effort and laughter, you finally have a moment of mental clarity. You realize that practicing meditation and deep breathing isn't just about clearing the mental fog—it's about finding humor in the human experience and laughing at life's distractions. You might not achieve instant zen master status, but you're okay with that. After all, life is a lot more fun when you're laughing at the Clarity Carnival of it all.

The Moral Of The Story

Engaging in practices that promote mental clarity and focus is a journey that promises to bring peace and understanding to your life. It might not always go according to plan, and there might be some comedic mishaps along the way, but the effort is what counts. So, keep breathing deeply, keep laughing, and keep finding joy in the midst of life's Clarity Carnival.

THE OPTIMISM OPUS

A Witty Guide to Embracing Life's Challenges with a Smile

Welcome to the Optimism Opus, where we'll take a humorous look at the art of embracing life's challenges with gratitude. Get ready for a comedic journey through the ups and downs of turning obstacles into opportunities for growth, all while maintaining a sense of humor along the way.

The Grateful Gambit Begins

You embark on your quest to practice gratitude for life's challenges, armed with optimism and a willingness to see the silver lining in every cloud. You envision yourself as a gratitude guru, effortlessly turning setbacks into stepping stones. But as soon as you encounter your first challenge—a flat tire on a rainy day—you find yourself cursing your luck and questioning the universe's sense of humor.

The Challenge Comedy

You attempt to practice gratitude, hoping to find the hidden blessings in difficult situations. But just as you start to see the light at the end of the tunnel, your cat decides to knock over a vase, adding insult to injury. You try to maintain your composure, but it's like trying to find peace in a house full of mischievous kittens.

The Gratitude Gauntlet

You try to embrace life's challenges with gratitude, recognizing them as opportunities for growth. But just as you start to feel a sense of appreciation for the lessons learned, your neighbor decides to throw a loud party that lasts well into the night. You try to focus on the positive, but it's like trying to find tranquility in the middle of a rock concert.

The Epiphany (Or Lack Thereof... Again)

After much effort and laughter, you finally have a moment of gratitude for life's challenges. You realize that practicing gratitude isn't just about being thankful for the good times— it's about finding humor in the tough times and laughing at the absurdity of it all. You might not achieve instant gratitude guru status, but you're okay with that. After all, life is a lot more fun when you're laughing at the Optimism Opus of it all.

The Moral Of The Story

Practicing gratitude for life's challenges is a journey that promises to bring resilience and strength to your life. It might not always go according to plan, and there might be some comedic mishaps along the way, but the effort is what counts. So, keep smiling, keep laughing, and keep finding joy in the midst of life's Gratitude Gala.

THE INTERCONNECTED
IMBROGLIO

A Hilarious Exploration of
Life's Cosmic Connections

Welcome to the Interconnected Imbroglio, where we'll take a humorous dive into the deep waters of existential contemplation. Get ready for a whimsical journey through the interconnectedness of all beings and the impact of your actions on others, sprinkled with a generous dose of cosmic comedy.

The Cosmic Conundrum Begins

You embark on your quest to reflect on the interconnectedness of all beings, armed with existential curiosity and a penchant for pondering the profound. You envision yourself as a contemplative sage, unraveling the mysteries of the universe with each thoughtful reflection. But as you sit down to ponder the cosmic web of life, your mind starts to wander like a lost tourist in a labyrinth.

The Interconnected Intrigue

You attempt to reflect on the interconnectedness of all beings, hoping to grasp the cosmic dance of cause and effect. But just as you start to feel a sense of enlightenment, your phone decides to ring with a call from a telemarketer offering you a once-in-a-lifetime opportunity to buy a timeshare on the moon. You try to ignore the distraction, but it's like trying to find inner peace in a crowded marketplace.

The Cosmic Comedy

You strive to engage in cosmic contemplation, seeking to understand your place in the grand tapestry of existence. But just as you start to connect the dots of the universe, your cat decides to join in with a series of meows that rival a philosophical debate. You try to maintain your focus, but it's like trying to find clarity in a room full of existential fog.

The Epiphany (Or Lack Thereof... Again)

After much effort and laughter, you finally have a moment of cosmic clarity. You realize that reflecting on the interconnectedness of all beings isn't just about understanding the universe—it's about finding humor in the cosmic chaos and laughing at the absurdity of it all. You might not achieve instant enlightenment, but you're okay with that. After all, life is a lot more fun when you're laughing at the Interconnected Imbroglio of it all.

The Moral Of The Story

Reflecting on the interconnectedness of all beings and the impact of your actions on others is a journey that promises to bring perspective and empathy to your life. It might not always go according to plan, and there might be some cosmic mishaps along the way, but the effort is what counts. So, keep reflecting, keep laughing, and keep finding joy in the midst of life's

TOPHER CAVA

Interconnected Imbroglio.

THE INTERRUPTION
INTERVENTION

A Comical Quest for Listening

Welcome to the Interruption Intervention, where we'll embark on a humorous journey through the practice of not interrupting. Get ready for a comedic exploration of conversation etiquette and the art of listening as we navigate the social seas with a chuckle and a nod to the urge to interject.

The Interruption Intervention Introduction

You step into the world of uninterrupted conversation, armed with a vow of silence and a nodding smile. You envision yourself as a listener extraordinaire, ready to resist the urge to interject with a quick quip or a witty remark. But as soon as you enter, your thoughts start to bubble up like a pot of popcorn on a hot stove.

The Interruption Intervention Temptation

You attempt to practice not interrupting, hoping to improve your listening skills. But just as you start to listen attentively, a temptation appears—a juicy tidbit of information that begs to be shared like a secret in a crowded room. You try to resist, but it's like trying to hold back a sneeze in a quiet library.

The Interruption Intervention Distraction

You try to practice not interrupting, recognizing the value of letting others speak. But just as you start to focus on the speaker, a distraction appears—a buzzing fly that demands your attention like a persistent salesman. You try to ignore it, but it's like trying to swat a fly in a tornado.

The Interruption Intervention Anticipation

You strive to practice not interrupting, understanding that patience is key. But just as you start to relax into the conversation, an anticipation appears—an itch of anticipation that begs to be scratched like a lottery ticket waiting to be scratched. You try to resist, but it's like trying to ignore an itch in a wool sweater.

The Interruption Intervention Triumph

After much effort and laughter, you finally triumph in the Interruption Intervention. You realize that practicing not interrupting isn't just about being polite—it's about finding humor in the urge to interject and laughing at the quirks of conversation. You might not always succeed in staying silent, but you're okay with that. After all, life is a lot more fun when you're laughing at the Interruption Intervention of it all.

The Moral Of The Story

Practicing not interrupting is a journey that promises to bring improved listening skills and better communication. It might not always go according to plan, and there might be some comedic mishaps along the way, but the effort is what counts.

So, keep practicing, keep laughing, and keep finding joy in the midst of life's Interruption Intervention.

THE WELL-BEING WHIRLIGIG

A Lighthearted Carousel of Self-Care

Welcome to the Well-Being Whirligig, where we'll embark on a humorous journey through engaging in well-being. Get ready for a merry-go-round of self-care strategies and laughter yoga as we spin through the realm of wellness with a smile and a spin.

The Well-Being Whirligig Entrance

You step into the whirligig of well-being, armed with a ticket of tranquility and a map of mindfulness. You envision yourself as a wellness warrior, ready to tackle the twists and turns of self-care with a serene smile and a sense of humor. But as soon as you take your first spin, your thoughts start to twirl like a top in a tornado.

The Well-Being Whirligig Temptation

You attempt to engage in well-being, hoping to nurture your mind, body, and spirit. But just as you start to unwind, a temptation appears—a sweet treat that beckons you with its siren song of indulgence like a dessert buffet at a diet convention. You try to resist, but it's like trying to ignore a craving for chocolate.

The Well-Being Whirligig Dizziness

You try to engage in well-being, recognizing the importance of balance and harmony. But just as you start to find your center, a dizziness appears—a whirlwind of thoughts that threatens to topple your tranquility like a spinning top on a wobbly table. You try to steady yourself, but it's like trying to find your balance on a rollercoaster.

The Well-Being Whirligig Relaxation

You strive to engage in well-being, understanding that relaxation is key to your health. But just as you start to unwind, a relaxation appears—a nap that calls to you with its promise of peace like a hammock on a sunny day. You try to stay awake, but it's like trying to resist a lullaby.

The Well-Being Whirligig Joyride

After much effort and laughter, you finally enjoy The Well-Being Whirligig. You realize that engaging in well-being isn't just about self-care—it's about finding joy in the journey and laughing at the twists and turns of life. You might not always find perfect balance, but you're okay with that. After all, life is a lot more fun when you're laughing at The Well-Being Whirligig of it all.

The Moral Of The Story

Engaging in well-being is a journey that promises to bring balance and joy to your life. It might not always go according to plan, and there might be some comedic mishaps along the way, but the effort is what counts. So, keep spinning, keep laughing, and keep finding joy in the midst of life's Well-Being Whirligig.

THE FORGIVENESS FESTIVAL

A Jocular Journey to Letting Go and Moving On

Welcome to the Forgiveness Festival, where we'll take a humorous stroll through the world of forgiveness. Get ready for a carnival of comedic mishaps and heartwarming breakthroughs as we explore the art of forgiving yourself and others, and releasing any lingering resentments.

The Forgiveness Festivities Begin

You set out on your quest for inner peace, armed with the intention to practice forgiveness. You envision yourself as a forgiving guru, spreading love and understanding like confetti at a celebration. But as soon as you try to forgive, your mind starts to replay past mistakes like a DJ with a broken record.

The Forgiveness Fiasco

You attempt to practice forgiveness, hoping to release any lingering resentments. But just as you start to let go, your inner critic crashes the party with a list of all your faults and failures. You try to silence the critic, but it's like trying to stop a parade with a kazoo.

The Forgiveness Fireworks

You try to forgive others, recognizing that holding onto grudges only weighs you down. But just as you start to feel a sense of freedom, the person you're trying to forgive does something that reignites your anger. You try to keep your cool, but it's like trying to put out a fire with a squirt gun.

The Forgiveness Fanfare

You strive to release any lingering resentments, understanding that forgiveness is a gift you give yourself. But just as you start to feel at peace, your dog decides to chase its tail in circles around you, disrupting the moment like a playful prankster at a serious ceremony. You try to regain your focus, but it's like trying to find serenity in a circus.

The Epiphany (Or Lack Thereof... Again)

After much effort and laughter, you finally have a moment of forgiveness. You realize that forgiving yourself and others isn't just about letting go of the past—it's about finding humor in the human experience and laughing at the absurdity of it all. You might not achieve instant forgiveness guru status, but you're okay with that. After all, life is a lot more fun when you're laughing at the Forgiveness Festival of it all.

The Moral Of The Story

Practicing forgiveness towards yourself and others is a journey that promises to bring peace and lightness to your life. It might not always go according to plan, and there might be some comedic mishaps along the way, but the effort is what counts. So, keep forgiving, keep laughing, and keep finding joy in the midst of life's Forgiveness Fiesta.

THE IMPERMANENCE INTRIGUE

A Whimsical Expedition into the Ever-changing Landscape of Life

Welcome to the Impermanence Intrigue, where we'll embark on a humorous journey through the ever-changing landscape of life. Get ready for a rollercoaster ride of comedic mishaps and profound realizations as we explore the impermanence of life and the importance of living in the present moment.

The Impermanence Inquiry Begins

You set out on your quest to reflect on the impermanence of life, armed with contemplative curiosity and a desire to embrace the present moment. You envision yourself as a zen master, calmly observing the ebb and flow of existence. But as soon as you try to focus on the present, your mind starts to wander like a lost tourist in a bustling market.

The Impermanence Illusion

You attempt to reflect on the impermanence of life, hoping to find peace in the midst of change. But just as you start to feel a sense of acceptance, your phone buzzes with a notification that pulls you back into the whirlwind of distractions. You try to ignore it, but it's like trying to find stillness in a hurricane.

The Impermanence Incognito

You try to embrace the impermanence of life, recognizing that everything is in a constant state of flux. But just as you start to surrender to the flow, your cat decides to knock over a vase, shattering the moment like a clumsy dancer at a ballet. You try to find your center, but it's like trying to find balance on a tightrope in a storm.

The Impermanence Insight

You strive to live in the present moment, understanding that the past is gone and the future is uncertain. But just as you start to savor the here and now, your neighbor decides to start a noisy construction project that shakes the foundation of your mindfulness. You try to stay grounded, but it's like trying to find peace in a construction zone.

The Epiphany (Or Lack Thereof... Again)

After much effort and laughter, you finally have a moment of clarity. You realize that reflecting on the impermanence of life isn't just about embracing change—it's about finding humor in the human experience and laughing at the absurdity of it all. You might not achieve instant zen master status, but you're okay with that. After all, life is a lot more fun when you're laughing at the Impermanence Intrigue of it all.

The Moral Of The Story

Reflecting on the impermanence of life and the importance of

living in the present moment is a journey that promises to bring peace and perspective to your life. It might not always go according to plan, and there might be some comedic mishaps along the way, but the effort is what counts. So, keep reflecting, keep laughing, and keep finding joy in the midst of life's Impermanence Intrigue.

THE SAVORY SENSATION

*A Comedic Exploration
of Mindful Eating*

W elcome to The Savory Sensation, where we'll embark on a humorous journey through the practice of savoring each bite of your food. Get ready for a deliciously funny adventure in mindful eating as we explore the flavors of the world with a smile and a sprinkle of culinary comedy.

The Savory Sensation Setting

You sit down to a meal, armed with a fork of focus and a spoonful of mindfulness. You envision yourself as a connoisseur of cuisine, ready to savor each morsel with a discerning palate and a dash of humor. But as soon as you take the first bite, your taste buds tingle with excitement, and your mind begins to wander like a chef in a bustling kitchen.

The Savory Sensation Temptation

You attempt to practice savoring each bite, hoping to fully appreciate the flavors. But just as you start to savor, a temptation appears—a tantalizing aroma wafts from the kitchen, tempting you to take another bite before you've fully savored the first like a dessert tray tempting a dieter. You try to resist, but it's like trying to ignore the smell of freshly baked cookies.

The Savory Sensation Distraction

You try to practice savoring each bite, recognizing the value of mindful eating. But just as you start to focus on the flavors, a distraction appears—a loud noise from the street that breaks your concentration like a fire alarm in a quiet room. You try to tune it out, but it's like trying to enjoy a peaceful meal during a parade.

The Savory Sensation Indulgence

You strive to practice savoring each bite, understanding that mindfulness can enhance your dining experience. But just as you start to indulge in the flavors, an indulgence appears —a craving for more that threatens to overshadow your appreciation like a dessert cart after a large meal. You try to resist, but it's like trying to resist a second helping of your favorite dish.

The Savory Sensation Satisfaction

After much effort and laughter, you finally achieve The Savory Sensation. You realize that practicing savoring each bite isn't just about tasting—it's about finding joy in the simple act of eating and laughing at the quirks of appetite. You might not always savor every bite, but you're okay with that. After all, life is a lot more delicious when you're laughing at The Savory Sensation of it all.

The Moral Of The Story

Practicing savoring each bite is a journey that promises to bring mindfulness to your meals and enhance your dining experience. It might not always go according to plan, and there might be some comedic mishaps along the way, but the effort is what counts. So, keep savoring, keep laughing, and keep finding joy in the midst of life's Savory Sensation.

THE WELLNESS WHIMSY

A Droll Adventure in Pursuit of Physical Well-being

Welcome to the Wellness Whimsy, where we'll embark on a humorous journey through the world of practices that promote physical well-being. Get ready for a hilarious romp of comedic mishaps and triumphant triumphs as we explore the art of exercise, healthy eating, and other delightful pursuits for a healthier you.

The Well-Being Wager Begins

You set out on your quest for physical well-being, armed with a yoga mat and a salad bowl. You envision yourself as a fitness guru, striking the perfect warrior pose while munching on kale with grace and determination. But as soon as you start your workout, your mind starts to wander like a lost yogi in a sea of downward dogs.

The Exercise Extravaganza

You attempt to practice exercise, hoping to strengthen your body and boost your mood. But just as you start to feel the burn, your favorite workout playlist decides to shuffle to a slow ballad, killing your motivation faster than a treadmill at full speed. You try to pump up the volume, but it's like trying to dance to a funeral march.

The Healthy Eating Hijinks

You try to eat healthy, recognizing the importance of nourishing your body with wholesome foods. But just as you start to enjoy your salad, a rogue piece of lettuce decides to catapult itself onto your neighbor's plate, sparking a food fight that rivals a scene from a slapstick comedy. You try to salvage the situation, but it's like trying to eat soup with a fork.

The Well-Being Whirlwind

You strive to engage in practices that promote physical well-being, understanding that a healthy body leads to a healthy mind. But just as you start to feel a sense of accomplishment, your cat decides to join in with a series of zoomies that turn your yoga session into a chaotic cat circus. You try to maintain your balance, but it's like trying to find stillness in a hurricane.

The Epiphany (Or Lack Thereof... Again)

After much effort and laughter, you finally have a moment of physical well-being. You realize that promoting physical health isn't just about exercise and healthy eating—it's about finding humor in the human experience and laughing at the absurdity of it all. You might not achieve instant fitness guru status, but you're okay with that. After all, life is a lot more fun when you're laughing at the Wellness Whimsy of it all.

The Moral Of The Story

Engaging in practices that promote physical well-being is a journey that promises to bring vitality and joy to your life. It might not always go according to plan, and there might be some comedic mishaps along the way, but the effort is what counts. So, keep exercising, keep eating healthy, and keep finding joy in the midst of life's Wellness Whimsy.

THE SELF-FORGIVENESS SHUFFLE

A Waggish Quest for Inner Peace

Welcome to the Self-Forgiveness Shuffle, where we'll embark on a humorous journey through the art of forgiving yourself for past mistakes and shortcomings. Get ready for a dance of comedic mishaps and heartfelt revelations as we explore the ups and downs of letting go and embracing self-compassion.

The Self-Forgiveness Soiree Begins

You step onto the dance floor of self-forgiveness, armed with a sense of humor and a willingness to embrace your imperfections. You envision yourself as a forgiveness maestro, gracefully moving through the steps of releasing guilt and shame. But as soon as you start to forgive, your inner critic decides to join the party with a playlist of your greatest hits of self-doubt, turning your dance into a comedy of errors.

The Self-Forgiveness Shuffle

You attempt to practice self-forgiveness, hoping to free yourself from the weight of past mistakes. But just as you start to let go, your mind starts to replay your most cringe-worthy moments on a loop, accompanied by a laugh track that echoes in your head like a sitcom gone wrong. You try to change the channel, but it's like trying to dance to two different songs at once.

The Self-Forgiveness Shenanigans

You try to forgive yourself for past mistakes, recognizing that you're human and bound to make errors. But just as you start to feel a sense of relief, your cat decides to knock over a lamp, casting a spotlight on your forgiveness process like a feline director in a slapstick comedy. You try to clean up the mess, but it's like trying to erase a mistake with an etch-a-sketch.

The Self-Forgiveness Samba

You strive to practice self-forgiveness, understanding that it's a process of letting go and moving forward. But just as you start to embrace your flaws, your dog decides to steal your socks and parade around the house like a sock thief in a parade. You try to catch him, but it's like trying to hold onto the past.

The Epiphany (Or Lack Thereof... Again)

After much effort and laughter, you finally have a moment of self-forgiveness. You realize that forgiving yourself isn't just about letting go of the past—it's about finding humor in the human experience and laughing at the absurdity of it all. You might not achieve instant forgiveness maestro status, but you're okay with that. After all, life is a lot more fun when you're laughing at the Self-Forgiveness Shuffle of it all.

The Moral Of The Story

Practicing forgiveness towards yourself for past mistakes and shortcomings is a journey that promises to bring freedom and lightness to your life. It might not always go according to plan, and there might be some comedic mishaps along the way, but the effort is what counts. So, keep forgiving, keep laughing, and keep finding joy in the midst of life's Self-Forgiveness Shuffle.

THE INTERCONNECTEDNESS INTERGALACTIC

An Entertaining Odyssey Through the Cosmic Dance of Life

Welcome to the Interconnectedness Intergalactic, where we'll embark on a humorous journey through the cosmic dance of life and the interconnectedness of all things. Get ready for a cosmic comedy of errors and cosmic revelations as we explore the interwoven tapestry of existence and your place in the cosmic web.

The Interconnectedness Inquiry Begins

You set out on your quest to reflect on the interconnectedness of all things, armed with a telescope to peer into the cosmos and a magnifying glass to examine the smallest details of life. You envision yourself as a cosmic detective, unraveling the mysteries of the universe and your place within it. But as soon as you start to contemplate the vastness of existence, your mind starts to wander like a lost astronaut in space.

The Interconnectedness Intrigue

You attempt to reflect on the interconnectedness of all things, hoping to find meaning in the cosmic dance of life. But just as you start to connect the dots, your phone buzzes with a notification that pulls you back into the earthly realm of distractions. You try to ignore it, but it's like trying to find silence in a symphony.

The Interconnectedness Incognito

You try to ponder the interconnectedness of all things, recognizing the beauty of the cosmic ballet. But just as you start to feel a sense of awe, a passing car honks its horn, disrupting your cosmic contemplation like a rude interruption at a meditation retreat. You try to regain your focus, but it's like trying to find serenity in a traffic jam.

The Interconnectedness Insight

You strive to reflect on the interconnectedness of all things, understanding that everything is connected in the grand tapestry of life. But just as you start to feel a cosmic connection, a bird decides to leave a surprise on your shoulder, grounding you back to earth like a practical joke from the universe. You try to clean up the mess, but it's like trying to tidy up after a hurricane.

The Epiphany (Or Lack Thereof... Again)

After much effort and laughter, you finally have a moment of cosmic insight. You realize that reflecting on the interconnectedness of all things isn't just about understanding the universe—it's about finding humor in the cosmic dance of life and laughing at the absurdity of it all. You might not achieve instant cosmic detective status, but you're okay with that. After all, life is a lot more fun when you're laughing at the Interconnectedness Intergalactic of it all.

The Moral Of The Story

Reflecting on the interconnectedness of all things and your place in the web of life is a journey that promises to bring awe and wonder to your life. It might not always go according to plan, and there might be some comedic mishaps along the way, but the effort is what counts. So, keep reflecting, keep laughing, and keep finding joy in the midst of life's Interconnectedness Intergalactic.

THE ABUNDANCE APPRECIATION

A Laughable Celebration of Abundance

Welcome to the Abundance Appreciation, where we'll embark on a humorous celebration of abundance in your life, both material and spiritual. Get ready for a joyous journey of comedic revelations and heartfelt appreciations as we explore the abundance around us and within us.

The Abundance Appreciation Gaiety Begins

You step into the grand hall of gratitude, adorned with streamers of appreciation and confetti of abundance. You envision yourself as the guest of honor, surrounded by the riches of life and the wealth of the heart. But as soon as you start to count your blessings, your mind starts to wander like a partygoer in search of the hors d'oeuvres table.

The Abundance Appreciation Glitch

You attempt to practice gratitude for the abundance in your life, hoping to cultivate a sense of appreciation. But just as you start to feel grateful, your phone rings with a call from a telemarketer offering you a once-in-a-lifetime deal on a timeshare in Antarctica, interrupting your moment of reflection like a cold call in the middle of a warm hug. You try to politely decline, but it's like trying to refuse a second helping of dessert.

The Abundance Appreciation Gaffe

You try to express gratitude for the abundance in your life, recognizing the richness of your experiences and relationships. But just as you start to feel a sense of warmth, your cat decides to knock over a vase, spilling water everywhere and dampening the mood like a wet blanket at a party. You try to clean up the mess, but it's like trying to dry off in a rainstorm.

The Abundance Appreciation Glitz

You strive to practice gratitude for the abundance in your life, understanding that it's not just about material wealth—it's about appreciating the small joys and simple pleasures. But just as you start to feel content, a gust of wind blows through the open window, scattering your gratitude list like confetti at a parade. You try to gather your thoughts, but it's like trying to catch a butterfly in a hurricane.

The Epiphany (Or Lack Thereof... Again)

After much effort and laughter, you finally have a moment of gratitude. You realize that practicing gratitude isn't just about counting your blessings—it's about finding humor in the human experience and laughing at the absurdity of it all. You might not achieve instant gratitude guru status, but you're okay with that. After all, life is a lot more fun when you're laughing at the Abundance Appreciation of it all.

The Moral Of The Story

Practicing gratitude for the abundance in your life, both material and spiritual, is a journey that promises to bring joy and contentment. It might not always go according to plan, and there might be some comedic mishaps along the way, but the effort is what counts. So, keep practicing, keep laughing, and keep finding joy in the midst of life's Gratitude Gala.

THE CREATIVITY CABARET

A Jovial Extravaganza of Self-Expression

Welcome to the Creativity Cabaret, where we'll embark on a humorous journey through the world of activities that nurture your creativity and allow you to express yourself. Get ready for a whimsical adventure of artistic mishaps and imaginative escapades as we explore the joy of creative exploration and self-expression.

The Creativity Cabaret Commences

You step onto the stage of creativity, adorned with a paintbrush in one hand and a ukulele in the other. You envision yourself as a creative virtuoso, effortlessly weaving a tapestry of colors and melodies. But as soon as you start to create, your mind starts to wander like a lost artist in a sea of blank canvases.

The Creative Chaos

You attempt to engage in activities that nurture your creativity, hoping to unleash your artistic genius. But just as you start to get into the flow, your phone buzzes with a notification that derails your creative train of thought like a conductor with a mischievous streak. You try to ignore it, but it's like trying to paint a masterpiece with a crayon.

The Creative Comedy

You try to nurture your creativity, recognizing the importance of self-expression and artistic exploration. But just as you start to feel inspired, your cat decides to walk across your keyboard, adding a touch of feline flair to your digital masterpiece. You try to shoo him away, but it's like trying to catch a rainbow in a net.

The Creative Carnival

You strive to engage in activities that allow you to express yourself, understanding that creativity is a journey of discovery. But just as you start to feel a sense of artistic freedom, a gust of wind blows through your window, scattering your art supplies like confetti at a parade. You try to gather your thoughts, but it's like trying to catch a cloud in a jar.

The Epiphany (Or Lack Thereof... Again)

After much effort and laughter, you finally have a moment of creative inspiration. You realize that nurturing your creativity isn't just about the end result—it's about finding humor in the creative process and laughing at the absurdity of it all. You might not achieve instant artistic virtuoso status, but you're okay with that. After all, life is a lot more fun when you're laughing at the Creativity Cabaret of it all.

The Moral Of The Story

Engaging in activities that nurture your creativity and allow you to express yourself is a journey that promises to bring joy and self-discovery. It might not always go according to plan, and there might be some comedic mishaps along the way, but the effort is what counts. So, keep creating, keep laughing, and keep finding joy in the midst of life's Creativity Cabaret.

THE UNIQUENESS UPROAR

A Humorous Romp Through the Quirks of Life

Welcome to the Uniqueness Uproar, where we'll embark on a humorous journey through the recognition that everyone is on their own unique journey. Get ready for a riotous adventure of quirky encounters and eccentric escapades as we explore the joy of embracing individuality and celebrating diversity.

The Uniqueness Unveiling

You step into the uproar of uniqueness, armed with a magnifying glass to examine the quirks of life and a rubber chicken to keep things light-hearted. You envision yourself as a connoisseur of eccentricity, appreciating the delightful oddities of human existence. But as soon as you start to observe, your mind starts to wander like a curious cat in a room full of mysteries.

The Uniqueness Uproar

You attempt to recognize that everyone is on their own unique journey, hoping to cultivate a sense of empathy. But just as you start to appreciate diversity, your phone rings with a call from a telemarketer offering you a lifetime supply of pickles, interrupting your moment of reflection like a pickle in a fruit salad. You try to decline politely, but it's like trying to explain quantum physics to a goldfish.

The Uniqueness Uproar

You try to recognize that everyone is on their own unique journey, recognizing the beauty of individual paths. But just as you start to feel a sense of unity, a bird decides to build a nest in your hair, turning you into a temporary aviary like a birdwatcher with a really bad hair day. You try to shoo it away, but it's like trying to untangle a ball of yarn.

The Uniqueness Uproar

You strive to recognize that everyone is on their own unique journey, understanding that each person's path is valid. But just as you start to embrace differences, a gust of wind blows through the uproar, scattering your understanding like confetti at a parade. You try to gather your thoughts, but it's like trying to catch a cloud.

The Epiphany (Or Lack Thereof... Again)

After much effort and laughter, you finally have a moment of recognition. You realize that recognizing that everyone is on their own unique journey isn't just about tolerance—it's about finding humor in the human experience and laughing at the absurdity of it all. You might not achieve instant recognition guru status, but you're okay with that. After all, life is a lot more fun when you're laughing at the Uniqueness Uproar of it all.

The Moral Of The Story

Recognizing that everyone is on their own unique journey is a journey that promises to bring understanding and unity. It might not always go according to plan, and there might be some comedic mishaps along the way, but the effort is what counts. So, keep recognizing, keep laughing, and keep finding joy in the midst of life's Uniqueness Uproar.

THE ADMIRATION AFFAIR

An Amusing Exploration of Personal Growth

W elcome to the Admiration Affair, where we'll embark on a humorous journey through the reflection on the qualities you admire in others and how you can cultivate them in yourself. Get ready for a whimsical adventure of self-discovery and character development as we explore the joy of embracing inspiration and aspiring to greatness.

The Admiration Adventure Begins

You step into the affair of admiration, armed with a mirror to reflect on your own potential and a telescope to gaze at the stars of inspiration. You envision yourself as an admirer of excellence, seeking to emulate the qualities that inspire you in others. But as soon as you start to admire, your mind starts to wander like a dreamer in a world of possibilities.

The Admiration Amusement

You attempt to reflect on the qualities you admire in others, hoping to cultivate them in yourself. But just as you start to envision your transformation, your phone buzzes with a notification that distracts you with cat videos, derailing your aspirations like a comedic interlude in a serious movie. You try to resist the temptation, but it's like trying to ignore a clown at a funeral.

The Admiration Absurdity

You try to cultivate the qualities you admire in others, recognizing the potential for growth and self-improvement. But just as you start to feel inspired, a bird decides to steal your pen and fly away, leaving you with a sense of loss and a newfound appreciation for feathered thieves. You try to retrieve it, but it's like trying to catch a feather in a hurricane.

The Admiration Acrobatics

You strive to cultivate the qualities you admire, understanding that it's a journey of self-discovery and personal development. But just as you start to make progress, a gust of wind blows through the affair, scattering your aspirations like confetti at a celebration. You try to gather them up, but it's like trying to collect stars in a cloudy night sky.

The Epiphany (Or Lack Thereof... Again)

After much effort and laughter, you finally have a moment of reflection. You realize that reflecting on the qualities you admire in others and how you can cultivate them in yourself isn't just about self-improvement—it's about finding humor in the human experience and laughing at the absurdity of it all. You might not achieve instant admiration guru status, but you're okay with that. After all, life is a lot more fun when you're laughing at the Admiration Affair of it all.

The Moral Of The Story

Reflecting on the qualities you admire in others and how you can cultivate them in yourself is a journey that promises to bring growth and self-discovery. It might not always go according to plan, and there might be some comedic mishaps along the way, but the effort is what counts. So, keep reflecting, keep laughing, and keep aspiring to greatness in the midst of life's Admiration Affair.

THE MINDFUL MAYHEM ON WHEELS

A Witty Spin on Staying Present Behind the Wheel

Welcome to the Mindful Mayhem on Wheels, where we'll embark on a humorous journey through the practice of mindfulness while driving, staying present and focused on the road. Get ready for a wild ride of traffic tantrums and highway hijinks as we explore the joy of staying centered behind the wheel and embracing the chaos of the open road.

The Mindful Mayhem Kickoff

You rev up for the mayhem of mindfulness, equipped with a steering wheel as your meditation mat and a rearview mirror as your portal to enlightenment. You envision yourself as a zen driver, navigating the chaos of rush hour with grace and poise. But as soon as you start to concentrate, your mind starts to wander like a GPS with a mind of its own.

The Mindful Mayhem Meltdown

You attempt to practice mindfulness while driving, hoping to stay present and focused on the road ahead. But just as you start to take deep breaths and relax into the flow of traffic, a car cuts you off, sending you into a fit of road rage that would make a traffic cop blush. You try to contain your fury, but it's like trying to put out a fire with a squirt gun.

The Mindful Mayhem Madness

You try to stay present and focused on the road, recognizing the importance of mindfulness in safe driving. But just as you start to find your zen, a squirrel darts across the road, causing you to swerve and honk your horn like a conductor in a symphony of chaos. You try to regain your composure, but it's like trying to herd cats in rush hour traffic.

The Mindful Mayhem Mix-Up

You strive to practice mindfulness while driving, understanding that it's not just about getting from point A to point B—it's about enjoying the journey. But just as you start to appreciate the scenery, a billboard advertises a sale at your favorite donut shop, tempting you to make an impromptu pit stop like a kid in a candy store. You try to resist the temptation, but it's like trying to ignore the smell of freshly baked cookies.

The Epiphany (Or Lack Thereof... Again)

After much effort and laughter, you finally have a moment of mindfulness. You realize that practicing mindfulness while driving isn't just about staying focused—it's about finding humor in the unexpected moments and laughing at the absurdity of it all. You might not achieve instant zen driver status, but you're okay with that. After all, life is a lot more fun when you're laughing at the Mindful Mayhem on Wheels of it all.

The Moral Of The Story

Practicing mindfulness while driving, staying present and focused on the road, is a journey that promises to bring calm and clarity. It might not always go according to plan, and there might be some comedic mishaps along the way, but the effort is what counts. So, keep driving, keep laughing, and keep finding joy in the midst of life's Mindful Mayhem on Wheels.

THE CLARITY QUEST

A Hilarious Expedition into
the Depths of Inner Peace

W elcome to the Clarity Quest, where we'll embark on a humorous journey through practices that promote mental clarity and focus, such as meditation and deep breathing. Get ready for a light-hearted adventure of inner exploration and tranquility turmoil as we delve into the joys of finding clarity amidst life's chaos.

The Clarity Quest Commencement

You embark on the quest for clarity, armed with a meditation cushion as your trusty steed and a mantra as your battle cry against distractions. You envision yourself as a zen warrior, ready to conquer the turbulent seas of your mind. But as soon as you close your eyes to meditate, your thoughts start to wander like a lost explorer in a labyrinth of distractions.

The Clarity Quest Conundrum

You attempt to practice meditation and deep breathing, hoping to find mental clarity and focus. But just as you start to breathe deeply and center yourself, your phone buzzes with notifications, pulling you back into the digital whirlpool like a fish caught in a net. You try to ignore it, but it's like trying to meditate in the middle of a circus.

The Clarity Quest Chaos

You try to promote mental clarity and focus, understanding the importance of inner peace in a hectic world. But just as you start to feel a sense of calm, a neighbor starts mowing their lawn, disrupting your serenity like a thunderstorm on a clear day. You try to block out the noise, but it's like trying to find silence in a rock concert.

The Clarity Quest Comedy

You strive to engage in practices that promote mental clarity, recognizing that it's a journey of self-discovery and tranquility. But just as you start to find your center, a fly buzzes around your head, landing on your nose at the most inconvenient moment like a persistent party crasher. You try to swat it away, but it's like trying to catch a cloud with your bare hands.

The Epiphany (Or Lack Thereof... Again)

After much effort and laughter, you finally have a moment of clarity. You realize that practicing meditation and deep breathing isn't just about finding focus—it's about finding humor in the human experience and laughing at the absurdity of it all. You might not achieve instant zen master status, but you're okay with that. After all, life is a lot more fun when you're laughing at the Clarity Quest of it all.

The Moral Of The Story

Engaging in practices that promote mental clarity and focus, such as meditation and deep breathing, is a journey that promises to bring peace and understanding. It might not always go according to plan, and there might be some comedic mishaps along the way, but the effort is what counts. So, keep breathing, keep laughing, and keep finding joy in the midst of life's Clarity Quest.

THE GRATITUDE GAMBIT

A Lighthearted Spin on Embracing Life's Challenges

Welcome to the Gratitude Gambit, where we'll embark on a humorous journey through the practice of gratitude for the challenges in your life, recognizing them as opportunities for growth. Get ready for a laugh-out-loud adventure of mishaps and triumphs as we explore the joy of embracing life's curveballs with a smile and a wink.

The Gratitude Gambit Launch

You set sail on the gambit of gratitude, armed with a journal as your treasure map and a positive attitude as your compass. You envision yourself as a gratitude guru, ready to turn life's lemons into lemonade with a dash of humor. But as soon as you start to jot down your first challenge, your pen runs out of ink like a quill in the hands of a forgetful scribe.

The Gratitude Gambit Giggle

You attempt to practice gratitude for the challenges in your life, hoping to see them as opportunities for growth. But just as you start to count your blessings, your cat decides to knock over your journal, spilling ink all over your carpet like a modern art masterpiece gone wrong. You try to clean up the mess, but it's like trying to mop up a waterfall with a sponge.

The Gratitude Gambit Guffaw

You try to recognize challenges as opportunities for growth, understanding the power of a positive mindset. But just as you start to see the silver lining, your neighbor's dog starts barking incessantly, disrupting your thoughts like a comedian bombing on stage. You try to ignore the noise, but it's like trying to sleep through a fireworks display.

The Gratitude Gambit Gag

You strive to embrace life's challenges with gratitude, knowing that they can lead to personal development. But just as you start to feel optimistic, your phone rings with a call from a telemarketer offering you a lifetime supply of rubber chickens, distracting you with absurdity like a clown at a funeral. You try to decline politely, but it's like trying to explain quantum physics to a goldfish.

The Epiphany (Or Lack Thereof... Again)

After much effort and laughter, you finally have a moment of gratitude. You realize that practicing gratitude for life's challenges isn't just about finding silver linings—it's about finding humor in the human experience and laughing at the absurdity of it all. You might not achieve instant gratitude guru status, but you're okay with that. After all, life is a lot more fun when you're laughing at the Gratitude Gambit of it all.

The Moral Of The Story

Practicing gratitude for the challenges in your life, recognizing

them as opportunities for growth, is a journey that promises to bring resilience and wisdom. It might not always go according to plan, and there might be some comedic mishaps along the way, but the effort is what counts. So, keep smiling, keep laughing, and keep finding joy in the midst of life's Gratitude Gambit.

THE RIPPLE EFFECT RUCKUS

A Comical Dive into the Puddle of Personal Influence

Welcome to the Ripple Effect Ruckus, where we'll embark on a humorous journey through the reflection on the impact of your actions on others. Get ready for a hilarious adventure of unintended consequences and serendipitous slip-ups as we explore the joy of understanding the ripple effect of our daily antics.

The Ripple Effect Ruckus Prelude

You dip your toes into the ruckus of reflection, armed with a mirror to peer into your soul and a magnifying glass to examine your influence on others. You envision yourself as a master of cause and effect, ready to navigate the waters of consequence with wit and wisdom. But as soon as you start to ponder, your mind drifts like a leaf on a windy day.

The Ripple Effect Ruckus Wobble

You attempt to reflect on the impact of your actions on others, hoping to see the bigger picture of your influence. But just as you start to connect the dots, your cat decides to knock over your magnifying glass, shattering your concentration like a bull in a china shop. You try to regain your focus, but it's like trying to catch a butterfly in a hurricane.

The Ripple Effect Ruckus Tumble

You try to understand the ripple effect of your actions, recognizing the interconnectedness of all beings. But just as you start to feel enlightened, a bird flies overhead and drops a surprise gift on your head, breaking your reverie like a slapstick comedy routine. You try to clean up the mess, but it's like trying to dry off in a monsoon.

The Ripple Effect Ruckus Bounce

You strive to reflect on the impact of your actions, understanding that every choice has a consequence. But just as you start to make connections, your phone rings with a call from a long-lost relative offering you a lifetime supply of rubber chickens, distracting you with absurdity like a circus in your living room. You try to decline politely, but it's like trying to explain gravity to a helium balloon.

The Epiphany (Or Lack Thereof... Again)

After much effort and laughter, you finally have a moment of reflection. You realize that reflecting on the impact of your actions on others isn't just about understanding consequences —it's about finding humor in the unpredictability of life and laughing at the absurdity of it all. You might not achieve instant enlightenment, but you're okay with that. After all, life is a lot more fun when you're laughing at the Ripple Effect Ruckus of it all.

The Moral Of The Story

Reflecting on the impact of your actions on others is a journey that promises to bring insight and empathy. It might not always go according to plan, and there might be some comedic mishaps along the way, but the effort is what counts. So, keep pondering, keep laughing, and keep finding joy in the midst of life's Ripple Effect Ruckus.

THE ATTENTION ABSURDITY

*A Whimsical Odyssey into the
Art of Uninterrupted Listening*

Welcome to the Attention Absurdity, where we'll embark on a humorous journey through the practice of giving your full attention to the speaker without interrupting. Get ready for a side-splitting adventure of verbal jousting and conversational chaos as we explore the joy of mastering the art of attentive listening without losing your mind.

The Attention Absurdity Prelude

You dive headfirst into the absurdity of attention, armed with earplugs to block out distractions and a notepad to jot down your thoughts. You envision yourself as a master of the mindful ear, ready to navigate the verbal minefield with grace and poise. But as soon as you start to focus, your mind starts to wander like a tourist in a maze.

The Attention Absurdity Juggle

You attempt to give your full attention to the speaker without interrupting, hoping to show your respect and understanding. But just as you start to listen intently, your phone buzzes with notifications, tempting you to check your messages like a kid in a candy store. You try to resist the urge, but it's like trying to ignore a siren's call.

The Attention Absurdity Tangle

You try to listen without interrupting, recognizing the importance of being fully present in conversations. But just as you start to engage, your friend launches into a long-winded story about their cat's latest antics, testing your patience like a marathon runner in a sprint. You try to stay focused, but it's like trying to corral a herd of unruly kittens.

The Attention Absurdity Tango

You strive to give your full attention, understanding that it's not just about hearing words—it's about truly listening. But just as you start to tune in, a loud noise outside your window breaks your concentration like a jackhammer in a library. You try to block it out, but it's like trying to meditate in the middle of a construction site.

The Epiphany (Or Lack Thereof... Again)

After much effort and laughter, you finally have a moment of attentive listening. You realize that giving your full attention to the speaker without interrupting isn't just about being polite—it's about finding humor in the quirks of human communication and laughing at the absurdity of it all. You might not achieve instant listening guru status, but you're okay with that. After all, life is a lot more fun when you're laughing at the Attention Absurdity of it all.

The Moral Of The Story

Practicing giving your full attention to the speaker without interrupting is a journey that promises to bring understanding and connection. It might not always go according to plan, and there might be some comedic mishaps along the way, but the effort is what counts. So, keep listening, keep laughing, and keep finding joy in the midst of life's Attention Absurdity.

THE THERAPY THEATRE

An Entertaining Curtain Call on the Stage of Self-Discovery

Welcome to the Therapy Theatre, where we'll embark on a humorous journey through the world of therapy. Get ready for a laugh-out-loud exploration of personal growth and introspective antics as we delve into the joys of engaging in therapy with a sense of humor and a dash of wit.

The Therapy Theatre Opening Act

You step onto the stage of self-discovery, armed with a therapist as your director and a script of your life as your script. You envision yourself as the star of your own show, ready to tackle the complexities of your psyche with grace and insight. But as soon as you start to delve into your issues, your mind starts to wander like a cat in a yarn factory.

The Therapy Theatre Drama

You attempt to engage in therapy, hoping to gain insight and clarity into your thoughts and feelings. But just as you start to open up, your therapist asks a probing question that catches you off guard, sending you into a fit of nervous laughter like a stand-up comedian bombing on stage. You try to regain your composure, but it's like trying to put out a fire with a water pistol.

The Therapy Theatre Comedy

You try to explore your inner workings in therapy, understanding that it's not just about solving problems—it's about understanding yourself better. But just as you start to make progress, your therapist suggests an unconventional exercise that leaves you speechless, like a mime in a thunderstorm. You try to follow along, but it's like trying to dance the tango on roller skates.

The Therapy Theatre Tragedy

You strive to engage in therapy, recognizing that it's a journey of self-discovery and healing. But just as you start to delve deeper, your therapist challenges you to confront a long-buried fear, sending you into a panic like a mouse in a maze. You try to face your fear, but it's like trying to wrestle a grizzly bear.

The Epiphany (Or Lack Thereof... Again)

After much effort and laughter, you finally have a moment of clarity. You realize that engaging in therapy isn't just about solving problems—it's about finding humor in the human experience and laughing at the absurdity of it all. You might not achieve instant enlightenment, but you're okay with that. After all, life is a lot more fun when you're laughing at the Therapy Theatre of it all.

The Moral Of The Story

Engaging in therapy is a journey that promises to bring insight and healing. It might not always go according to plan, and there might be some comedic mishaps along the way, but the effort is what counts. So, keep exploring, keep laughing, and keep finding joy in the midst of life's Therapy Theatre.

BOOKS BY THIS AUTHOR

The Scenic Route To Happiness: 101 (Not So) Serious Paths To Finding Real Happiness

Get ready to laugh, reflect, and find real joy with this unique and enjoyable guide!

Embark on a whimsical journey to lasting bliss with "The Scenic Route to Happiness: 101 (Not So) Serious Paths to Real Happiness." This delightful guidebook is your ticket to a joy-filled life, offering a collection of offbeat and unexpectedly entertaining routes to finding true contentment. From the quirky to the profound, these 101 unconventional paths will have you laughing, pondering, and discovering the simple, profound truths that lead to lasting happiness. So, buckle up, toss your expectations out the window, and join us on the scenic route to a brighter, more joyful existence!

Laugh Together, Love Together: 101 Budget-Friendly Date Ideas That Will Make Him (And You) Smile

Discover a world of romance with 101 wallet-friendly date adventures that promise laughter, love, and lasting memories and are sure to sweep your husband or boyfriend off his feet!

Embark on a journey of laughter, love, and adventure with Laugh Together, Love Together. This delightful step-by-step guide is your ticket to creative, free or inexpensive date nights that are sure to spice up your relationship. Whether you're a seasoned couple looking to add some spice to your routine or a new pair eager to explore together, these 101 budget-friendly date ideas are guaranteed to inspire laughter, romance, and endless fun. From quirky DIY projects to offbeat outdoor escapades, each idea is a delightful twist on traditional romance. Say goodbye to boring dates and hello to a whole new level of excitement with this witty and practical guide to affordable romance!

Laugh Together, Love Together: 101 Budget-Friendly Date Ideas That Will Make Her (And You) Smile

Discover a treasure trove of romantic adventures with 101 wallet-friendly date ideas, guaranteed to charm your wife or girlfriend with laughter, love, and unforgettable memories, all while removing the stress of planning and execution! Even if you try just one of these unique dates each month, you'll be set for over eight years without having to brainstorm your own ideas!

Embark on a journey of laughter, love, and adventure with Laugh Together, Love Together. This helpful and fun to read step-by-step guide is your ticket to creative, free or inexpensive date nights that are sure to spice up your relationship. Whether you're a seasoned couple looking to add some spice to your routine or a new pair eager to explore together, these 101 budget-friendly date ideas are guaranteed to inspire laughter, romance, and endless fun. From quirky DIY projects to offbeat outdoor escapades, each idea is a delightful twist on traditional romance. Say goodbye to boring dates and hello to a whole new level of excitement with this witty and practical guide to affordable romance!

Printed in Great Britain
by Amazon

41118750R00169